A *Glorious* CHURCH

A Glorious Church. Copyright © 2020. C. Orville McLeish. All Rights Reserved.

No rights claimed for public domain material, all rights reserved. No parts of this publication may be reproduced, stored in any retrieval system, or transmitted in any form or by any means, electronic, mechanical, recording, or otherwise, without the prior written permission of the author. Violations may be subject to civil or criminal penalties.

ISBN: 978-1-949343-71-7 (paperback)
　　　978-1-949343-72-4 (eBook)
　　　978-1-953759-16-0 (hardback)

Printed in the United States of America

2nd Edition

A Glorious CHURCH

In Pursuit Of The Biblical Model Of Christianity

C Orville McLeish

Foreword by Rev. Valentine Rodney

I want to dedicate this volume to the memory of one of my favourite cousins, who died tragically on 02.02.2020.

He is the first person who died during my pursuit of God, and the real, true church that I really desired to raise from the dead.

Visit:

www.corvillemcleish.com

for more books and articles that will help you on your faith journey.

Foreword

Thought-provoking and challenging, this manuscript opens the door for a frank and open conversation on the scriptures. It is evident that the author believes that much diligence is applicable in the search for truth, and that truth can stand the test of scrutiny and re-examination.

C. Orville is not asking you to blindly embrace his conclusions, but rather to take the journey with him using the various tools available to analyze the scriptures. He makes the clarion call that the modern-day Church needs to be committed to the model clearly outlined in scriptures, both by precept and example. He is bold in his assertions, many of which may result in a paradigm shift or present the need for further thought and research.

One cannot deny his passion to see in this era an awakening of the believer and by extension the Church. As you read, be prepared to be challenged, encouraged and edified, as you embark on this journey to see what is, the Glorious Church.

Rev. Valentine Rodney, Author
Director Word Impact Ministries International

Table of Contents

Foreword 9

Acknowledgements 13

Introduction 15

CHAPTER ONE: Sons of God 17

CHAPTER TWO: Repairing the Breach 29

CHAPTER THREE: Why Am I Here 41

CHAPTER FOUR: Faith 55

CHAPTER FIVE: Defeating Fear 69

CHAPTER SIX: Our Natural Habitat 83

CHAPTER SEVEN: Suffering in Silence 95

CHAPTER EIGHT: God Still Speaks 111

CHAPTER NINE: Christ in Us 123

CHAPTER TEN: The Power of a Transformed Mind 135

CHAPTER ELEVEN: Maximize Your Potential 145

CHAPTER TWELVE: Back to the Garden of Eden 159

CHAPTER THIRTEEN: A Glorious Church 167

CHAPTER FOURTEEN: As He Is, So Are You 179

Conclusion 193

Acknowledgements

Firstly, I must give thanks to my Father, who continues to teach me the ways of a son. He has enlightened me and brought me into a working knowledge of who I am in Him. I seek only to know Him more, so I can make Him known.

Thanks to my Brother and Lord, Jesus, who has stayed with me even during the darkest seasons of my life. Now that I look back, I see Him more clearly than I have ever seen before and know that even when I thought He had abandoned me, He never did.

Thanks to my very soft-spoken and invisible Guide, Holy Spirit, who leads me in such a calm and almost natural way. I have found that even with the simplest of chores, He teaches me and enables me to do things I had no prior knowledge of, like writing a book. Without Him, none of this would be possible.

I thank my family and friends who support my vision and take the time to listen to the revelations I receive.

I give honour and special recognition to my mentor and spiritual father, Dr. O, through whose teachings and guidance, a lot of my doctrine and what I believe have been challenged and corrected. I now read the Bible with fresh eyes.

Finally, many thanks to the love of my life, Nordia, who supports me in such a way that crowns everything I do with excellence.

Introduction

There are two reasons this book had to be written, the first is the powerlessness of most of our churches: the second, the faithlessness of most Christians. I believe Father God wants to address these issues because of what He is doing in the earth today. He is calling for a cohesiveness among all churches worldwide as He has gently whispered in my spirit that *the part is not the whole*. This book is just a part, you reading it is just a part, what He has called you to do is just a part. The true miracle takes place when all the parts come together as one.

Jesus asked a relevant question in Saint Luke 18:8: *"...When the Son of man comes, will he find faith on earth?"*

In Ephesians Chapter 5 we read: *"For husbands, this means love your wives, just as Christ loved the church. He gave up his life for her to make her holy and clean, washed by the cleansing of God's Word. He did this to present her to himself as **a Glorious Church** without a spot or wrinkle or any other blemish. Instead, she will be holy and without fault."* Verses 25-27 – NLT (emphasis mine).

We need to get back to our roots. Jesus Christ is the example for every believer to follow. He is the standard of normal Christian living, and anything less is unacceptable and renders His sacrifice null and void. He promised the Father to present to Him a 'glorious Church' free from blemishes, and that is exactly what He will do.

We need to get back to the model church that He established with His life, death and resurrection.

We need to become the Acts 29 church...A glorious Church, a people of faith...a perfect church, who will pick up the mantle where Jesus and the Apostles left off after bringing to ruin the kingdom of darkness. I am amazed that we have managed over the centuries to give power back to everything that Jesus disempowered through His ministry.

At the end of each Chapter is a Prophetic Word I believe I received in my spirit from God over the course of writing this book.

CHAPTER ONE
Sons of God

This will probably be the most controversial of all Chapters in this book. When this revelation came, I was blown away, but not dissuaded as somehow a lot of things just started to make sense. So, if you are ready to know who you are, then read on.

I have never been the kind to just accept what other people say. I realized very early on that the Bible is open to various interpretations, and very often we accept what makes sense to us and preach that as a fixed doctrine. Later, when new revelations come, we are hesitant to let go of old beliefs because it will cause us to face our shortcomings as human beings prone to err. No one wants to admit that they were wrong.

Revelation will always come to the one who is not afraid to admit that what they believed was wrong.

One of the issues I have always had a particular problem with was the Scriptures found in Genesis 6:2 & 4:

"That the sons of God saw the daughters of men that they were fair, and they took them wives of all which they chose. There were giants in the earth in those days; and also after that, when

the sons of God came in unto the daughters of men, and they bare children to them, the same became mighty men who are of old, men of renown."

Several red flags go up when I read these Scriptures. The most obvious question is, "Who are sons of God?" It is a pertinent question that has been answered for centuries by renowned Biblical scholars who claimed that sons of God are angels or fallen angels. I had several issues with that answer. Firstly, the Bible has never been hesitant to refer to angels as angels, so why on this particular and seemingly isolated instance would the Word refer to angels as sons of God? The second issue I have, and the most pertinent, is that angels or demons cannot reproduce with humans. To put it bluntly, a spirit cannot ejaculate human sperm to impregnate a woman. Only physical creatures have the capacity to reproduce.

With that said, there is a heavy cloud of mystery surrounding 'sons of God.' The term 'sons of God' appears only nine other times in Scripture, six of which are in the New Testament. I think it is necessary to quote those verses here:

"Now there was a day when the sons of God came to present themselves before the Lord, and Satan came also among them." - Job 1:6

"Again there was a day when the sons of God came to present themselves before the Lord, and Satan came also among them to present himself before the Lord." - Job 2:1

A Glorious Church

"When the morning stars sang together, and all the sons of God shouted for joy?" - Job 38:7

"But as many as received him, to them gave he power to become the sons of God, even to them that believe on his name." - St. John 1:12

"For as many as are led by the Spirit of God, they are the sons of God." - Romans 8:14

"For the earnest expectation of the creature waiteth for the manifestation of the sons of God." - Romans 8:19

"That ye may be blameless and harmless, the sons of God, without rebuke, in the midst of a crooked and perverse nation, among whom ye shine as lights in the world." - Philippians 2:15

"Behold, what manner of love the Father hath bestowed upon us, that we should be called the sons of God: therefore the world knoweth us not, because it knew him not." - 1 John 3:1

"Beloved, now we are the sons of God, and it doth not yet appear what we shall be: but we know that, when he shall appear, we shall be like him; for we shall see him as he is." - 1 John 3:2

Bear in mind that previous interpretations, or what I was asked to believe, is that in the Old Testament 'sons of God' were fallen angels, and in the New Testament 'sons of God' referred to humans.

C. Orville McLeish

To know the truth, we sometimes have to travel back to the beginning. Armed with all my confusion, and revelation received from others I went to take a look, and what I found was surprising (to say it mildly).

"In the beginning God created the heaven and the earth." - Genesis 1:1

What we read in Genesis Chapter 1 has always been attributed to, by and large, what was happening in the earth, in the natural, but let's take a closer look.

"And God said, let us make man in our image, after our likeness: and let them have dominion over the fish of the sea, and over the fowl of the air, and over the cattle, and over all the earth, and over every creeping thing that creepeth upon the earth." - Genesis 1:26

"So God created man in his own image, in the image of God created he him; male and female created he them." - Genesis 1:27

When we get to Genesis 2:5 it says:

"And every plant of the field before it was in the earth, and every herb of the field before it grew: for the Lord God had not caused it to rain upon the earth, and there was not a man to till the ground."

You will understand that by this point I was utterly confused, but what I missed was that before there was anything on the earth, it had to be created first in the heavens. That is why we read "and God created the heavens and the earth."

"So God created man in his own image, in the image of God created he him; male and female created he them." - Genesis 1:27

Both male and female were created in the image and likeness of God, so we looked like God. We bore His resemblance. Note also that both male and female were created before God formed man from the dust, and before Eve was taken out of Adam, that is if you read the sequence of events in chronological order. Theologians will say that Genesis 1 is a summary, and Genesis 2 expands on the summary. If that was true, both chapters read like a summary, so there would be some overlapping which makes very little sense.

"And the Lord God planted a garden eastward in Eden; and there he put the man whom he had formed." - Genesis 2:7

In Genesis 2, everything that God created in the realm of the spirit took form in the natural, including man and woman. We were now spirit (Genesis 1), soul and body (Genesis 2), and we looked like God: we were a living soul so we must have looked way different from how we look now. I believe this is why it was possible for them to be naked and unashamed (See Genesis 2:25). I have heard it said by theologians that a celestial light covered man. It was not just light, but who they were – who we are.

The dynamics of man, however, changed when we sinned. When Adam sinned, his soul died leaving the body exposed. He knew this was going to happen because he was already seeing it happen with his wife.

> *"May God himself, the God of peace, sanctify you through and through. May your whole **spirit, soul and body** be kept blameless at the coming of the Lord Jesus Christ."* - 1 Thessalonians 5:23

Some believe we are a body with a soul and spirit inside when the truth is we are a soul/spirit being, with a body.

Look at this verse:

"And Adam lived an hundred and thirty years, and begat a son in his own likeness, after his image; and called his name Seth." - Genesis 5:3

Mankind no longer resembled God but became a reflection of our fallen natural man. We were a body with a dead soul, but we still had the breath of God (Spirit). In essence, we really died on that day Adam and Eve disobeyed God and fell into sin.

As a spirit being, you were initially a son of God who stood before the throne of God, even shouted for joy when stars begun to sing before his throne (See Job 38:7). Every human being was a son of God before being conceived in this world. You were a son of God before conception, and it doesn't matter the circumstance that brought you here.

"Before I formed thee in the belly I knew thee; and before thou camest forth out of the womb I sanctified thee, and I ordained thee a prophet unto the nations." - Jeremiah 1:5

Jesus made a very startling statement about Himself in John 3:13:

No one has ascended into heaven except he who descended from heaven, the Son of Man.

We would have no rights to go back to heaven (ascend), if we did not descend from heaven. We are born from above (See John 3:3). "Born again" is not in the original language of the Bible. The correct term is "born from above" or "born from heaven." This revelation also explains pre-destination because every human being was pre-destined to be a son of God. Our names were already written in the book of life as an heir to the throne, but the choices we make while we are here will determine if our name remains or get blotted out. This is why I believe evangelism is so very important to God. We must remind His sons and daughters who they are, so they find their way back home, and not be lost to Him forever.

"He that overcometh, the same shall be clothed in white raiment; and I will not blot out his name out of the book of life, but I will confess his name before my Father, and before his angels." - Revelation 3:5

The fact that your name can be blotted out suggest that it is already written. I shared this revelation with a trusted few, and was shown an excerpt from a book that I want to quote here to make a point:

"Theory of pre-existence. This view, which advocates that the human soul has existed previously, has its roots in non-Christian philosophy; it is taught in Hinduism and was also held by Plato, Philo, and Origen. This theory teaches that in a previous existence man were angelic spirits, and as punishment and discipline for sin, they were sent to indwell human bodies. There are a number of problems with this view: there is no clear statement of Scripture to support this view (although the idea may have been presented in John 9:2); no one has any recollection of such an existence…"[1]

That last statement is no longer true. People undergoing generational deliverance have had the experience of remembering leaving heaven to be born on earth. There is a faint notion of truth embedded in a deception. I have found that is exactly how the enemy works from the beginning: he takes the truth and manipulates it to keep us from ever venturing near the truth. Almost everything that the enemy has distorted we have shunned out of fear or mere skepticism. In our state of ignorance, the enemy has established his kingdom here on earth unchallenged.

Keep in mind, however, a very simple truth: we are only born here on earth once; we only get to live life on earth once. God

---

[1] Paul P. Enns, *The Moody Handbook of Theology*, rev. and expanded. ed. (Chicago: Moody Publishers, ©2008), 317.

is not in the business of recycling, so this in no way supports reincarnation.

I had a very uncomfortable experience recently while away from home in a foreign country. I had been taking communion almost every night for several weeks. I was in the process of meditation and prayer when I suddenly felt my body start to literally enlarge. It was growing big, and very heavy and I thought I was going to die. I could sense the spirit of fear and death in the room but wasn't sure what was happening. No one has been able to explain this unfortunate episode, and that has been my issue with the church for years. I always ask the hard questions, but seldom get good answers. I look around me, and everyone is sick and having challenges. We are so focused on our physical bodies that we miss the reality of who we really are. Jesus became our sin and curse to redeem us. When we say yes to Jesus, our soul is made new, and that should be our focus. All that was paid for at the cross is contained within our new soul and must be released into every other area of our being for us to experience the abundant life that the Scriptures speak about.

On the other end of the spectrum, if you have never accepted Jesus as your Lord and Saviour, I need you to know today that you were born to be a son of God, not a sinner. Your place is with God, and every possible thing that would keep you away from God is deeply cloaked in deception. The enemy wants you to believe that you are living at the top of your game when in reality he is only robbing you of what is rightfully yours.

"The enemy comes to steal, kill and destroy; but I (Jesus) have come that you might have life, and have it more abundantly."
- John 10:10 (emphasis mine).

Can you truly say you are living an abundant life? Or is there this nagging impression that something very meaningful, and more fulfilling is missing from your life? I have met many people who are living a kind of life they don't want their children to live. In the same way, you have dreams for your kids, God has dreams for you. Everything He has ordained you to be and do is recorded on your scroll in heaven. This may all sound strange to you, but I believe you know it to be true.

I guess you have one very important question at this point. If you were a son of God, who stood before God's throne before you were formed in the womb, why can't you remember? Several things come to mind when I consider this question. I believe babies are born very innocent in this world and can see very clearly in the spirit, but as they grow, and are exposed to sin, they develop preconceived ideas and practice iniquity that lessens, and eventually destroys their ability to see in the spirit, unless they are reborn. If babies could talk, a lot of the mysteries we are seeking after now would be solved. On another note, we have never really asked the Father to help us remember. People have asked and have remembered. Maybe if you ask, He will grant that request. Finally, when we are born from above, we are reborn as a babe in Christ. Just as in the natural, a baby desires sincere milk as it grows. You would be surprised at how malnourished the souls of many

Christian's are due to negligence. In the same way, our physical body must be properly fed and nourished to grow, our soul demands the same effort. Even Jesus grew in stature, and wisdom and in favour with God and man (See Luke 2:52). You will also notice that there is something in every man that draws him to worship something. There will always be that part of us that knows its true home.

You were born to be a son of God. Rise up and take your place. Everything that Jesus accessed during His earthly ministry belongs to you. He wasn't just doing it for you, but He was demonstrating what God has placed inside you, and what you can do because of your sonship. Everything that Jesus did, you can do, and you are supposed to be doing before moving on to even greater things. That is the essence and purpose of this book, to activate you through knowledge and revelation to begin to walk like Jesus.

Go make your Father proud!

Prophetic Word

Before you were formed in the womb, I knew you. You were with Me. I know what you looked like, and how you sounded. I knew you. It is not a coincidence that you are reading this book. I found a willing hand and heart who would write this so that you can get this in your hand. Without a willing heart and hand, My Words go unsaid. But I consider it a privilege to be able to speak to you directly. I love you. Don't doubt. Don't be afraid. I know My thoughts towards you, they are thoughts of peace, health and prosperity, to give you an expected end. I have dreams for you, as a father dreams for his children. You are My son, and there are only two types of sons: the son who stays, and the son who strays, but they are both sons nonetheless. Come to Me, and let Me teach you who you really are; let Me show you who I really am.

CHAPTER TWO
Repairing the Breach

Those from among you shall build the old waste places; You shall raise up the foundations of many generations; And you shall be called the Repairer of the Breach, The Restorer of Streets to Dwell In. - Isaiah 58:12 - NKJV.

The dark side of society is deeply rooted in the foundations of past and present generations. Of even greater concern is the fast deteriorating standards of morality. Men love darkness more than light, and we have spread that darkness all over the earth. Every generation is taught to believe that the former was unnecessarily uptight in one matter or another; thereby killing society's conscience gradually.

We are victims of circumstances of our own making. There is a measure of hostility inherited by our younger generation through what they see at home, mass media content, social media networks, even video games! We have handed over the fate of our younger generation's destiny, to technological gadgets. Their perception of reality and truth is developed from whatever these gadgets throw their way. We choose to bury our heads in the sand when they are seemingly gravitating towards the "dark side." Beside failing to discipline them, we defend them as though they are victims of injustice, when they are corrected by others. Their filthy curses entertain us, we threaten those who dare to oppose them, without weighing the cause. We have abandoned our younger generations to raise themselves and learn of their own accord. We are already reaping the seeds we sew into these young lives. Every assassin, gunman, thief, prostitute, homosexual, etc. was once a child; a vulnerable ground where the seed of vice was sown without scrutiny. By the time they got to their teenage years, most of them were already living a fragmented life; being one person at home, and quite another outside home. Inevitably, the person outside home, will come home to haunt us.

Even if tomorrow, the church emerged in all its glory, there would still be deeply rooted issues haunting the generations. To heal the society, it will take more than spectacular miracles; healing all who are sick, delivering those who are oppressed, causing the lame to walk, the blind to see, the dumb to hear and raising the dead. It will take a concerted, deliberate effort from several generations to repair the breaches. This is is why I believe that, whatever we impart in the children born today, is paramount to raising a new earth from the ashes of what it is today.

The prophet Isaiah gives a practical approach to the solution:

"Cry aloud, spare not; lift up your voice like a trumpet; tell My people their transgression, and the house of Jacob their sins. Yet they seek Me daily, and delight to know My ways, as a nation that did righteousness, and did not forsake the ordinance of their God. They ask of Me the ordinances of justice; they take delight in approaching God. 'Why have we fasted,' they say, 'and You have not seen? Why have we afflicted our souls, and You take no notice?' "In fact, in the day of your fast you find pleasure, and exploit all your laborers. Indeed, you fast for strife and debate, and to strike with the fist of wickedness. You will not fast as you do this day, to make your voice heard on high. Is it a fast that I have chosen, a day for a man to afflict his soul? Is it to bow down his head like a bulrush, and to spread out sackcloth and ashes? Would you call this a fast, and an acceptable day to the Lord? "<u>Is this not the fast that I have chosen: to lose the bonds of wickedness, to undo the heavy burdens, to let the oppressed go free, and that you break every yoke? Is it not to share your bread with the hungry, and that you bring to your house the poor who are cast out; when you see the naked, that you cover him, and not hide yourself from your own flesh? Then your light shall break forth like the morning, your healing shall spring forth speedily, and your righteousness shall go before you; the glory of the Lord shall be your rear guard.</u> Then you shall call, and the Lord will answer; you shall cry, and He will say, 'Here I am.' "If you take away the yoke from your midst, the pointing of the finger, and speaking wickedness, if you extend your soul to the hungry and satisfy the afflicted soul, then your light shall dawn in the darkness, and your darkness shall be as the noonday. The Lord will guide you continually, and satisfy your soul in drought, and strengthen your bones; you shall be like a watered garden, and like a spring of water, whose waters do not fail." (Isaiah 58:1-11 – NKJV – emphasis mine).

There is a reason God told the Israelites to teach all they learned to their children, and to their children's children. The coming generation will inherit their perception of reality from us and I am not talking about generational curses and issues of the bloodline. How much darkness or light the next generation is born into is determined by our choices.

Allow me to use a fictitious character to illustrate how the former generation affects the latter. Meet Curtis A. Brown.

Curtis is born under unfavorable circumstances. His father abandoned his mother when she was pregnant. He did not play any significant role in their lives. Curtis' mother had to work two to three jobs to make ends meet, because she did not have a formal education. You see, she was born of a teenager who was unable to provide financially for her. Laying with men for handouts was how Curtis' grandmother provided for his mother. Curtis' mother had to run away from home to escape her abusive stepdads, only to end up living with a man who was no different from what she was running away from. She got pregnant with Curtis and was abandoned by the father shortly thereafter.

Curtis' mom did her best to send him to school. However, he did not have any good role model. His perception of life, therefore, was still skewed. He believed that the only purpose in life is to survive, hook or crook. Besides, that is what everyone he knew was doing. Curtis did not see the value of education. Afterall, his teachers did not care much, they only taught for a salary, not to change lives. He then turned his attention to girls, in order to affirm his manhood. He keeps himself well-groomed and is big on hygiene because that's what the girls like. He also assumes somewhat of a "bad boy" demeanor, because good guys don't get the girls. The girls don't understand why they are more attracted to the "bad boy"; it has to do with their perception of life as well.

As expected, Curtis graduated with nothing but his good looks and a cell phone. His pursuit of women still continued, but not for long before he realized that responsibility is inevitable. He realized that as girls grow into their womanhood, their preference changes from wanting a good looking 'bad boy' to wanting a man who can provide for their needs. So, now Curtis needs a job, but he is not qualified for the corporate world; he ended up working minimum wage jobs at a gas station, supermarket and a construction site. He was fixated on his deep sited need to find approval of his manhood from the ladies. He, therefore, spent his money trying to impress the ladies, rather than furthering his studies for a better job.

Now, consider this; if Curtis ever finds himself unemployed or dissatisfied with his earnings, then the temptation to seek "other" ways of making money arises. Considering his struggle with identity, lack of education, skewed perception of reality and weak moral foundation, it would be quite easy for Curtis to morph into an armed robber. He may shoot a man coming from work and leave with all his cash. But that man is somebody's husband, friend, uncle, father, brother, son. Yet another family will be left without the guidance of a father, and the cycle continues.

C. Orville McLeish

There are many variables to consider in this scenario, which go back several generations. The only hope for Curtis is if he identifies the loop of choices and dire consequences; and finds the courage to make different choices. One right choice can change the trajectory of the generation that follows, like the ripple effect of dropping a stone on a lake. We cannot change the past, but we can repair the breaches in our society; one good choice after another. Every right choice we make in the present is a seed of light sown, that will grow into a lighthouse beacon for generations to come.

The starting point is to acknowledge the existence of God. We must acknowledge we are here because God took the time to form us into being and placed us here. The idea that there is no God makes no sense in the grand scheme of things. We cannot measure or fathom existence because it extends beyond the boundaries of our mortal minds. We see the stars, moon, sun, other big lights that we assume are planets, but that is as far as we can see; we do not know what is beyond what we see and how far it stretches. Are there any limits, any boundaries, any end? I believe the physical creation is entombed in boundless unmeasurable time called eternity. It is like a measurable pod inside an immeasurable space. Mankind seems to be at the epoch of creation, because God became Man to redeem man. If our value is measured by the life of the Creator, who demonstrated a willingness to subject Himself to the cruelty of the hearts of His own creation, then we must be very important to Him. Acknowledging God and His sovereign superiority to us is the first step to repairing the breach. In so doing, we activate the light and nature that is intrinsic in man; having been created in God's image.

Once we activate our light by receiving Jesus Christ as Lord and Savior over our lives, and by allowing His Word and principles to govern our own lives, we can move on to shining that light as a beacon of direction and hope for creation. Every choice we make, no matter how small, will affect our reality, and our future. That thing we will experience twenty years from now could very well be the fruit of a seed that we plant today.

Embedded in nature are spiritual laws and principles that govern all creation. A seed, for example, has to die before it sprouts with life. Just like the seed, we have to die to our selfish and ignorant ways, get buried with Christ in baptism and rise up to newness of life. The seed then grows and matures before it produces fruit. Likewise, we too must grow and mature to bring forth fruit. The full potential of a fruitful tree is embedded in the seed, and it is brought forth through nurture in a conducive environment.

Every child that comes into this world starts as a seed and has the potential to be a child of God. The foundation of all the ills and vices in the world, is rejecting God and His seed within humanity. The further away we drift from the "original intention" of God in bringing man into existence, the more we contribute to spreading darkness over the earth. We cannot reject light without embracing darkness, for darkness is simply the absence of light.

In the beginning God created the heavens and the earth. The earth was without form, and void; and darkness was on the face of the deep. And the Spirit of God was hovering over the face of the waters. (Genesis 1:1-2 - NKJV).

The first thing God said was, "Let there be light" (See Genesis 1:3). This is not the physical light of the sun, moon or stars; those were created later. This is a different kind of light; divine light radiating from God's own nature. Jesus then came and said He is the light of the world (See John 8:12), and those who follow Him would have the light of life. Then He says you are the light of the world (See Matthew 5:14). We are the bearers of Light in this world. Our light radiates or diminishes with every choice that we make.

God has positioned believers in every crevice and corner of society, from the poorest communities to the richest, but our light is congealed because of fear and unbelief. If we are to become repairers of the breach, we must cast off all fear and unbelief and walk the ancient path of faith. This requires that we reject all doctrines of men and hold fast to the Biblical principles of life, even if our reality seems to contradict it. We must pursue what we know to be true, even if we are riddled with disappointment because our faith is not yet producing any tangible results.

Curtis, for instance, would need to take the first bold step in activating the light within his being. He could then make decisions that would have a positive impact on the future. He could decide to brave the temporary discomfort of ditching his girlfriends and going back to school at the expense of his ego, in order to build a career for himself and his dependants. Curtis could choose to tap into the gifting within him (everyone has at least one gift) and maximize on it for both profit and impact.

Teachers within our schools need to understand that they have a part to play. They can't just step into this vital role for money. They must understand that, similar to parents and guardians, they are the most important agents of change in the lives of the children placed under their tutelage. Children, all the way through their college years, spend more time at school than they do at home. Schools therefore bear the greater responsibility in raising a sober generation than even our churches.

Despite their busy schedules, parents need to give their time and energy into instilling good values in their children. They must be keen to extend this love and guidance to other children who may not be their own. That neighbour's child whose plight or little vice you ignored, could be the adult who robs and kills your own child or family member years later. The world really does function by the laws of karma (cause and effect). Every teen or adult who has embraced "darkness", is a manifestation of a missed opportunity by someone to make a positive impact during their childhood.

The parent-child relationship must move beyond 'dos' and 'do nots'. Children must understand the reason behind anything they are instructed about. They must understand motive; the fuel behind every action. There is a motive or a reason behind everything that we do.

Peer pressure is a perpetuation of false identities. It often stems from adolescents trying to find themselves. The view that a child develops of the world will go a far way into aiding their decision-making processes in adulthood. Children must learn the sanctity and value of life; and that conflicts are not best resolved through violence and hatred. The sooner they learn this, the better. They may be picked on at school or labeled as "soft", but they should be taught that restraining oneself from reacting to evil is actually one of the biggest strengths one could ever have! I speak more about the intrinsic "good and evil" embedded in our being in my book: ***Identity: Restored, Revealed, Initiate.***

Having been born and raised at a dispensation of abundant knowledge, this generation is called to repair the breaches in our society. It will take more than just a supernatural move of the Holy Spirit; we have a part to play through practical application of principles guided by God's Word and the Holy Spirit. It is all well and good that we can heal the sick, and raise the dead, but the world demands far more than a showcase of spectacular physical miracles in order to be truly healed. It requires practical rectification in Biblically guided acts that can be summed up in one word: love.

Jesus said to him, "'You shall love the Lord your God with all your heart, with all your soul, and with all your mind.' This is the first and great commandment. And the second is like it: 'You shall love your neighbor as yourself.' (Matthew 22:37-

39 - NKJV).

If God is love, then the one who radiates love activates his or her own divinity. This is how we partake of God's nature and attributes; this is how we reveal God to a world in crisis; this is how we expand our light to diminish darkness. Love is our true power, and the means by which we begin to repair the breaches. As the Apostle Paul says it, love is the more excellent way.

CHAPTER THREE
Why Am I Here

I struggled with that question for many years. My life, for the most part, has always felt a bit surreal and disjointed, as if I am caught between two worlds. On one hand, I could perceive and see very clearly the real, physical world, but it felt like a shadow of the real thing. It was hard to comprehend that the real world could not be seen with the physical eyes, or not easily perceived through the physical senses. This made it difficult, as my day-to-day life had a feeling as if I was being tugged in two different directions. It was within one of these surreal moments while driving, that I really began to ponder this question, "Why am I here?"

Why Am I Here?

We have all asked that question, haven't we? It sounds like a simple question that should have a simple answer. But I struggled with it for a moment and over the next few days or weeks, it evolved. It practically took on a life of its own, so I think it is fitting that as we consider our purpose on Earth as God's Church, we must seek an answer to this timely question.

We go to church from time to time and find ourselves pumping each other to worship. I am beginning to think we don't fully understand why we are here, who brought us here and where we are going. People who know and understand who they are, and whose they are, don't need to be pumped or given a reason to worship.

In addition to that very profound question, we may also find ourselves asking some supplemental questions such as, "Is there a purpose for our existence?" or "What is the significance of life?"

As a church, we agree with Solomon when he said the whole duty of man is to "serve God and keep his commandments," but why do we need to do that? Why should we serve God? There must be more to life than just church.

In Jeremiah 1:4-10 we read:

"Then the word of the Lord came unto me, saying, 'Before I formed thee in the belly I knew thee; and before thou camest forth out of the womb I sanctified thee, and I ordained thee a prophet unto the nations.' Then said I, Ah, Lord God! Behold, I cannot speak: for I am a child. But the Lord said unto me, Say not, I am a child: for thou shalt go to all that I shall send thee, and whatsoever I command thee thou shalt speak. Be not afraid of their faces: for I am with thee to deliver thee, saith the Lord. Then the Lord put forth his hand, and touched my mouth. And the Lord said unto me, Behold, I have put my words in thy mouth. See, I have this day set thee over the nations and over the kingdoms, to root out, and to pull down,

and to destroy, and to throw down, to build, and to plant."

We live in a day when people of all ages are dying, from a little child to the elder and every age in between. Twenty-year-olds are having heart attacks; children are being brutally slain and abused. There seems to be no end to evil and death. At some point in all our lives, we are going to have to grieve the death of a loved one, and if we live long enough, many people we know will die. This is a fact. None of us have control over who stays and who goes. But there must be someone in control, right? Who decides our fate? Who determines the seasons, and times; when the rain falls and when there will be droughts?

There's an elderly church couple that I admire very much, and recently, in a very short and unexpected moment, the husband died. As the widow grieved, she said, "I told him I wanted to go first." I remember my wife telling me that as well, so my question is, "Who decides in a marriage union who goes first, and who stays?" Surely there is someone making all those decisions. We don't really believe that life just happens, right? So what is the significance of life?

Many years ago, one of my church mothers preached a message and in it, she said, "We live to die." That sounds really discouraging and sad. We may even be forced to think there is nothing in life to look forward to but death. Many years ago, prior to the dreaded the year 2000, I had a choice and could return to school to do additional studies, and I thought, "Why bother? God will come by the year 2000." He didn't. I grew up fearing death and thinking that I would die young. I didn't die, but that thought process impacted my life in a very negative way. I could have done more with the time I wasted thinking I would not live to see age thirty. In the process, I abused my body with food and ended up paying the price for that as I grew older.

The future is uncertain and unpredictable, and we make poor choices sometimes. In our own eyes, we somehow think our sole purpose in life is to survive and acquire. *Survive and Acquire.* We build our lives and base our decisions on these two concepts:

- Survive the economic crisis.
- Survive in a crime-infested community.
- Survive our deteriorating health.
- Acquire more money, so we can do more, buy more, live more.
- Acquire a house, a nice car, nice clothes, and nice food.

We expend all or most of our energy into surviving and acquiring. We work long hours. We go to school while working long hours. We often get caught in a lifelong cycle of working and going to school as simply a means to an end.

Sometimes our happiness and contentment are dependent on how well we survive and how much we are able to acquire. For many, that is all there is to life. The downside to this mentality is that while surviving and acquiring, we put value on things and not ourselves. In our own eyes, we become insignificant and worthless because:

- We don't have enough.
- We don't talk proper English.
- We can't drive a car or own a house.
- We can't get a good job.
- We can't get a decent husband or wife.
- We are not smart.
- We can't read very well.

In Jeremiah 1:5, God says to the Prophet:

"Before I formed thee in the belly I knew thee; and before thou camest forth out of the womb I sanctified thee, and I ordained thee a prophet unto the nations."

Jeremiah was just a young boy when God first spoke these words to him. He was born in a time when there was nothing good going on in Israel, and the people were very hostile to God, though *hostile* may be a major understatement where the Israelites were concerned. They rejected God so consistently that He said:

'When you lift up your hands in prayer, I will not look. Though you offer many prayers, I will not listen...'

In my humble opinion, that's a bad place to be. There were other prophets in those days prophesying peace and victory, but God was not speaking through those prophets. God spoke through Jeremiah and what he said was completely different from what all the other prophets were saying, so the hostility of the people was extended to Jeremiah. Initially, he didn't handle that hostility well and even said he wished that he was not born. That's not a good place to be either.

We can learn from Jeremiah's life that we don't need to be saying what everybody else is saying. We don't need to be wearing what everybody else is wearing. "Before I formed you, I knew you…I sanctified you…I ordained you."

So this verse had me thinking about science. Though it may be a bit graphic, I think there is a point worth making. We know how this works. We don't talk about it, but we know. When a man and a woman come together and have sex, and the man ejaculates inside a woman, there are 30 – 60 million sperm in that one batch of semen. It only takes one sperm to make a human being. Each sperm contains a unique DNA and fingerprint. If any of the other 30 to 60 million sperm had come in contact with your mother's egg, you would not be here. Somebody else would have come forth with a different DNA, different fingerprints, maybe a different gender, and different facial features. But God wanted you. "Before I formed 'you' in the belly I knew 'you'…" God chose you to be born into this world. Your parents had no control over that. They did what they needed to and hoped for the best. The final decision was out of their hands. That means you are literally, "One in a million."

If you are not a Christian, and you are reading this book, you need to know that you are not here by some random accident. God chose you. For every soul that is conceived, even the

A Glorious Church

babies that are aborted, they can never cease to exist again. You will exist for all eternity, and that is why your decisions in life matter. You will understand why in some circumstances the Scripture says, "It would have been better for you if you were not born." It is a process and a reality that cannot be reversed once conception has taken place.

Can I speak to some confused young people? Even if your parents were just messing around; even if you are the product of fornication or adultery; even if your conception was an accident or was not planned for…out of 30 to 60 million possibilities…God chose you…He sanctified you…He ordained you. He gave you a name. Unless God changes your name, then that is the name you will have for all eternity. Suppose Larry decided that God made a mistake, and he should have been a woman. He spends millions of dollars and has a sex change and endures all that discomfort and pain. Then he goes to all the necessary government agencies and changes his name from Larry to Lorna. In God's eyes, he is still Larry. I believe that when Lorna dies, on resurrection day, it will be Larry standing before Jesus, and not Lorna. When God chose you out of 60 million possibilities, He did not make a mistake. He wanted you!

So the relevant question now is not, "Why am I here?" but "Why was I chosen?"

There was a time in history right after God had just formed man that He practically lived with man. He enjoyed a certain level of fellowship walking with man in the beautiful garden of Eden, but Adam and Eve messed up that relationship. Yes,

God could have just destroyed us and labeled our creation a failed scientific experiment, but there was just something about man that God loved and wanted to keep in spite of sin.

The Psalmist says:

"What is man that you are mindful of him, the son of man that you care for him?" - Psalm 8:4

God wanted to restore that broken relationship, but there was a problem: God required a blood sacrifice to atone for man's sin, and there was no sacrifice worthy enough. Many animals lost their lives in a futile attempt to restore the relationship between God and man, or to maintain it. All the major and minor prophets could attest to that. It got so bad that they were still making sacrifices, but their hearts were even further away from God.

God knew that there was only ONE worthy enough to be sacrificed as atonement for our sins. God was the only worthy sacrifice. He loved us that much.

John 3:16 says it perfectly:

"For God so loved the world, that He gave His only begotten Son. That whosoever believeth in Him should not perish, but have everlasting life."

Here is a bonus for you in John 3:17:

"For God did not send His Son into the world to condemn the world, but to save the world through Him."

Now that's talking about you and me. God literally rose from His eternal throne, took off His eternal robe, stepped from His eternal home and became one of us, so He could die for all us.

Philippians 2:5-8 says:

"Let this mind be in you, which was also in Christ Jesus: Who, being in the form of God, thought it not robbery to be equal with God: But made himself of no reputation, and took upon him the form of a servant, and was made in the likeness of men: And being found in fashion as a man, he humbled himself, and became obedient unto death, even the death of the cross."

If you are experiencing guilt and condemnation over some sin that you have committed, you need to understand that before God left heaven to come to earth, He saw you sinning and He died for you anyway. As a church, we sometimes give the impression that God only loves us when we do the right thing or when we get saved, but I have learned that God loves the prostitute and the gunman in the streets as much as He loves me. As a matter of fact, the Word teaches that when they get saved, they will love God more than I do, for the one who is forgiven much will love much.

I love God, but I don't know what it means to live on the streets or sell my body to survive. I don't know what it feels like to carry a gun, take someone's life or be addicted to drugs. My wife says I was born at the foot of the cross. I don't know about that, but I know God can deliver you from anything because nothing is impossible for Him. The point is, out of 30-60 million possibilities, God chose each of us, and He died for each of us.

But why would God die for us? Surely He doesn't need us to be God. Surely His existence would continue without us. Surely we are nothing for Him to care so much for us.

That is where we have it backward. Salvation is not about us going to God. It is about God coming to us. As sinners, we don't care about reconciling any relationship with God. We don't care about Him. We don't give Him any thought. He is the one trying to reconcile a broken relationship with man. This book, this life, everything you know about God is because of His attempts to reach us, and not the other way around. Naturally we are hostile towards Him. Some of you still are, but He loves you, and that's a fact that cannot be denied or debated, though we try. Atheists deny God's existence because they come face to face with Him. *It is impossible to deny the existence of something that doesn't exist.* Most of you will be reading that several times; I pray the Holy Spirit reveals the truth of that statement to your heart.

God wants to dwell with man on a new earth, and each of us was chosen as a potential resident of that new city.

John lived a remarkable life as the disciple who couldn't die. He wrote:

"I saw the Holy City, the new Jerusalem, coming down out of Heaven from God, prepared as a bride beautifully dressed for her husband." - Revelation 21:2 – NIV

Jesus said, "I go to prepare a place for you, that where I am there you will be also." A city made by God, just for us. Our true citizenship is on the new earth with God. We were individually handpicked by God out of millions of possibilities for a reason. We are all handpicked for eternity.

If we spend our appointed years chasing after our own selfish ambitions and never being reconciled to God, we will miss that city. We will miss the better part of eternity. We all go somewhere when we die.

So, Why Am I Here?

We were chosen as potential residents for that city being prepared for those who will accept what God has done on our behalf. I love the way Peter says it:

"But you are a chosen people, a royal priesthood, a holy nation, a people belonging to God, that you may declare the praises of him who called you out of darkness into his wonderful light." - 1 Peter 2:9

We were all specifically and deliberately chosen by God as one of the millions He wants to spend eternity with. This is why we come to church and why we witness to others with the hope that they will get saved. This is why we pay our tithes and give offerings. We have a reason to worship Jesus. We did not choose Him, but He chose us. (See John 15:16) Because He chose us, He says:

"Whatever you ask in my name the Father will give you."

That is a promise to the true church, which brings us to the purpose of this book. Many of us have had that unfortunate experience where we have asked God for something in the Name of Jesus, and nothing happens. We have even developed theologies and doctrines around those unfortunate experiences, and some of us don't even try to attain the standard of faith by which Jesus lived.

It was Bill Johnson of Bethel Church in Redding, California, who said, "Disappointments should never determine belief." We struggle with several issues as a church. For example, we might think, "If Jesus is the same yesterday, today and forever (Hebrews 13:8), why am I not seeing the same things He did when he walked this Earth?" or "He is still here, isn't He? If these signs shall follow those who believe (Mark 16:17-20), where are the signs?" Maybe even, "I have laid hands on the sick, and they have not recovered! I have tried to cast out a demon, and he practically laughed at my attempts." Or maybe you have thought, "I have never seen anyone raised from the dead, or the blind see, or the deaf hear, or the lame walk. What strange theology is this that contradicts our reality? Why would we be asked as a church to start believing in what we have never seen?"

Those are good questions. We need faith, real faith to bring us into an awareness of a reality that exists simultaneously with our observable reality, but better and perfect. Of course, it will contradict with our present reality. What hope would we have if they were both the same? Fortunately, what is seen is temporary and what we don't see will last forever. We have settled and conformed to the reality of our present world, but as God's Church, we are called to a greater reality, a reality that will change everything.

Prophetic Word

I have a few questions for you, says the Lord. Did you have any control over you coming into this world? Could you have chosen what sex you would be? Could you feed yourself while in your mother's womb? During the first year of your life, were you able to care for yourself? Do you even remember? I have cared for you all your life. When you weren't even thinking about Me, I was dying on your behalf. I shielded you, provided for you, blessed you and kept you through some very dark times. Do you really think you can survive this world without me? Yet you question me. Can the clay question the potter, and dictate anything to Him? My hand is on your life because I want to bring you into a full knowledge of who you really are. Every test that I have allowed in your life was designed to build you. Don't ask for the test to be removed but pray for the strength to endure. It is through the test that you will be established and confirmed. It is through the test that your identity as a son will be realized. Nothing about you surprises Me, so stop whining and complaining. Why not be thankful? I told you I would never leave you, and I meant it. You might not be able to perceive my presence, but I am there. I have always been there. I made you, I formed you, I know how to take care of you. You belong to me. Why are you here, you may ask? You are here because I wanted you to be here.

CHAPTER FOUR
Faith

"There are boundless possibilities for you, if you dare to believe."
—Smith Wigglesworth

The life of Smith Wigglesworth was one of faith. he never wavered, and he never doubted. From the moment he was baptized with Holy Spirit, he accepted the mantle of divine authority and power, and walked this earth like Jesus doing the same things, and even greater. But Smith Wigglesworth, a man who raised over a dozen people from the dead, was just a natural man like you and me. What he did, we can also do. he had the same Spirit that raised Jesus from the dead, and so do we. I believe that what separates us is faith. Let us begin with a few faith Scriptures:

"Now faith is confidence in what we hope for and assurance about what we do not see." - Hebrews 11:1 – NIV

"Consequently, faith comes from hearing the message, and the message is heard through the word about Christ." - Romans 10:17 – NIV

C. Orville McLeish

"For we live by faith, not by sight." - 2 Corinthians 5:7 – NIV

"And without faith it is impossible to please God, because anyone who comes to him must believe that he exists and that he rewards those who earnestly seek him." - Hebrews 11:6 – NIV

Faith is the currency of heaven. It is the means by which the reality of the Kingdom of God can be brought into our reality, literally bringing the culture of heaven to earth. What is the Kingdom of God? It is a kingdom of power, not talk (See 1 Corinthians 4:20) There is no sickness or lack in heaven, and we can live in that liberty, but only through faith.

I meditate on faith at all times. I can't seem to think about anything else. In my sleep, I can feel faith in my inner man, in my stomach. There is an expectation that something great is coming. Nothing new, but something great.

There was a time in history when a man walked this earth. His name is Jesus. He had a mission. He was the chosen Lamb, who would take away the sins of this world. But He was sent to accomplish an even greater purpose. He was to show man how to live on earth, thereby establishing the true *church*. Today, if we compare what the church is and what it was or was supposed to be, we can see that something went wrong somewhere in the history of the church. Today we talk, but there is no power, and that is not who the church is. As a matter of fact, there is no real Biblical reference for what we call church today. It is not Biblical and seems to be a culture that

A Glorious Church

was formed sometime after the Bible was written. Why we have grown comfortable with this powerless culture is beyond comprehension. While we do *church,* we simultaneously declare that we are the church and the Bible is our guide and final authority on all we think, do and believe. I guess this would be true if Jesus did not come.

The truth is, what we have now is no different from the synagogues Jesus came to challenge. They were places of tradition and rituals, with leaders who refused to change or conform to any other truth. We sing songs without contemplating the meaning of the words. If we do contemplate, we still sing with absolutely no intention of living the thoughts that leave our mouth.

I'll go where You want me to go, dear Lord, O'er mountain, or plain, or sea;
I'll say what You want me to say, dear Lord, I'll be what You want me to be.[2]

We even close our eyes in holy reverence while we utter the words of this song, but when asked to do, say or go, our answer is usually no. No one wants to go.

It can be confusing to witness how terribly inconsistent our actions are to what we say. Our lives seem to be out of sync. We think something, say something else and do something entirely different from what we think and say. Can you imagine

---
[2] I'll go Where You Want Me to go Mary Brown, 1891

anything more confusing that one life being pulled in three different directions? No wonder there is no power in our church. The only supernatural experience we can speak about is speaking in tongues, but even that has been brought into question. How can one individual get up and speak three words over and over again, and then give an interpretation that consists of a whole paragraph, or multiple sentences? It just doesn't add up.

The problem, though, is that we have done this for so long, and gotten so comfortable that we missed the fact that the true nature of the church would actually be needed in this time. Many are being tortured by demons, many are sick, many are dying before their time, and the church seems powerless to change the outcome. Jesus messed up every recorded funeral He attended. People died, and He raised them from the dead. People die today, and the church buries them all. That seems a little inconsistent with Scripture:

> *"Heal the sick, raise the dead, cleanse those who have leprosy, drive out demons. Freely you have received; freely give."* - St. Matthew 10:8 – NIV

The most we seek for is a commitment from sinners at the altar that they will serve God. It goes in the records, and they are abandoned to their own conscience soon after. The culture that exists as the church today is one where you leave the same way you entered. For a healthy bunch, this may be acceptable. But what about those who are sick, even terminally, and are told by a hospital that they must wait three years to do an operation that they need now because of an overcrowded schedule? You must admit, a church that has no power is a church without good news for those who need it. People want options. They want deliverance. They are seeking for something more, a greater reality that they may have read about in the Bible. Have we forgotten that it was once a reality? A Man walked this earth, and doctors and hospitals were almost out of work. He healed all who were sick and oppressed. All! The Disciples and Apostles did the same thing. They healed many. If we were even healing some, we should not be comfortable.

Here is a reality check for us all. A couple years ago depression was the leading mental disorder among the population. Now, anxiety has taken the lead, which is a condition rooted in fear. Why are people so consumed by fear? Wouldn't you be fearful if you know the possibility exists that at some point in your life you may be diagnosed with a terminal disease, and knowing your only options are doctors, medication to suppress symptoms while destroying something else, hospitals that are short staffed by employees who don't really care because they are now overcrowded and find it impossible to attend to the needs of everyone? In five years, with no active faith, you better be able to afford a private hospital as public hospitals will not have room to accommodate you, regardless of what is wrong with you. If the five-fold ministry and the demonstration of the power of the Holy Spirit do not return to our present day reality, we are going to be in big trouble.

I don't know what happened between Malachi and Matthew

(400 years of silence between the Old and New Testament), but when Jesus came, there seemed to be only a handful of righteous people. The church had become a synagogue of Satan. Jesus delivered a demon-possessed man who was sitting in the back of the church. We seemed to have gone full circle back to that level of oppression and bondage. We send our young people to retreats and camps to be delivered from demons but do nothing to close the many open doors in our lives. Church members are in blatant malice with each other, we take jobs that require us to lie and be deceitful, and we have sex outside of marriage. There are married men and women having sex with their spouse while imagining that they are sleeping with someone else. Pornography sites are accessed by the thousands per second worldwide, including Christians and including ministers. Homosexuality and lesbianism are practiced in secret, even within the church. Our people need deliverance. Our people need to be healed. If we remain on this course, we will be utterly destroyed.

A few years ago, I was in bondage to pornography and masturbation. I didn't want to be shackled to this sin, but I could not help myself. There was a deep hunger and thirst in me for it that could only be satisfied by daily practice. I was so deep in the practice that I honestly believed that if God could set me free from it that, He can do it for anyone. I never stopped going to church. Every Sunday, I went to the altar for deliverance, and every Sunday I went home and fell into the same sin. I remained undelivered. Despite the many prayers and petitions being offered on behalf of the needy at the altar, we went home the same. Nothing changed. Nothing moved.

Nothing left. It was a very confusing time in my life because I sincerely believed the church could do something about my condition. After all, that is what we preach. I stopped going to the altar. What was the use? It wasn't working. My church could not deliver me. This is the reality for a lot of people. Imagine their disappointment when the God who created all things is unable to help them because of their faithlessness. This reality is utterly embarrassing. If we save, but cannot deliver, our fruit will not remain. The statistics are rather frightening: only one out of every five persons who get baptized remains.

God eventually delivered me from my addiction, but not through the church. He delivered me through my relentless pursuit of Him, through the Word of God that cleanses, changes, renews, strengthens and establishes.

Jesus healed every sickness and disease. That was the standard He set, and it was supposed to be a part of the gospel that was spread throughout the world: the Good News:

*"Then the disciples went out and preached everywhere, and the Lord worked with them and confirmed his word by the **signs** that accompanied it."* - Mark 16:20 – NIV

What happened? Who made the choice to keep the theory and vanquish the practical side of the good news? Everyone who knows what it means to be sick will care about what is being said right here. If you are absolutely healthy, it may mean nothing to you.

We need to cross over. We cannot stay on this side of Jordan. I heard a message that totally blew me away by a Bishop at a recently concluded Camp Meeting of one of our sister churches. There were two tribes of Israel that disobeyed God when told to cross over Jordan to the land promised to them. They were the tribes of Rueben and Gad, Gad specifically. All the other tribes crossed over, except those two.

Later, when Jesus came, He went to the land they had chosen to occupy. He was met at the entrance by a man who was possessed by legions of demons. Jesus cast out those demons, who went into a herd of pigs and jumped off a cliff. The people of that land asked Jesus to leave, and they were never spoken of again; a lost tribe possessed and forgotten. They were lost because they never crossed over.

Jesus asked a very profound question that we need to pay attention to:

"When the Son of man comes, will He find faith on earth?" - Luke 18:8

So let's talk about faith, not as a word we utter meaninglessly, but a word that provokes action. The Scriptures say we are to be *'doers'* of the Word and not *'hearers'* only, but what does that look like?

There are two different types of faith, and I would not want us to confuse them. There is the *Gift of Faith.* This is a supernatural level of faith that is a gift of the Holy Spirit (See

1 Corinthians 12:9). This is not the faith every believer must practice. There is another faith, *saving faith.* This faith is what we acted on to be saved. This faith is what we exercised when we received the baptism of the Holy Spirit. This is the same faith that propels us into a supernatural lifestyle. The same faith that saved you can empower you to see and do the impossible. Most Christians never improve their faith beyond that point. Every Christian should exercise this faith. Like a muscle, it gets stronger and bigger with use, and eventually, our feet get planted on an irreversible course to experience God:

"from faith to faith." - Romans 1:17

Hebrews 11:6 says:

"...without faith it is impossible to please God."

In other words, there is just one way to please God. So here is an analogy that I want you to keep in mind. I went to the gym for a while, and I began to lift weights. My arm was big, but it was all fat. The first days of lifting weights, the muscles in my arm became sore to the point that I could hardly do anything. Eventually, there was no more pain, but my arm was still fat. After months of working out, one day I felt my arm, and it was solid. I was also stronger. I could not do one pushup before, and I could now do several. That happens when you work your muscle. The same thing happens when you work your faith.

C. Orville McLeish

Three Levels of Faith

I want to share a story with you that highlights three levels of faith. I believe each of us fall into one of these categories. It is always good to be able to identify where we are, and where we need to be.

Let's read Matthew 14:22-33 from the World English Bible:

"Immediately Jesus made the disciples get into the boat, and to go ahead of him to the other side while he sent the multitudes away. After he had sent the multitudes away, he went up into the mountain by himself to pray. When evening had come, he was there alone. But the boat was now in the middle of the sea, distressed by the waves, for the wind was contrary. In the fourth watch of the night, Jesus came to them, walking on the sea. When the disciples saw him walking on the sea, they were troubled, saying, "It's a ghost!" and they cried out for fear. But immediately Jesus spoke to them, saying "Cheer up! It is I! Don't be afraid." Peter answered him and said, "Lord, if it is you, command me to come to you on the waters." He said, "Come!" Peter stepped down from the boat, and walked on the waters to come to Jesus. But when he saw that the wind was strong, he was afraid, and beginning to sink, he cried out, saying, "Lord, save me!" Immediately Jesus stretched out his hand, took hold of him, and said to him, "You of little faith, why did you doubt?" When they got up into the boat, the wind ceased. Those who were in the boat came and worshiped him, saying, "You are truly the Son of God!"

In this story, we identify three levels of faith:

1. Those who walk on water like Jesus. It was early in the morning, and here comes Jesus walking on water as if it was solid ground under His feet. This is the highest level of faith.

2. Those who take a few steps before sinking like Peter. Note carefully how this Scripture is worded. The Scripture says Peter was afraid and started to sink. Jesus said, "You of *little faith*, why did you doubt?" Jesus equates doubt to fear. Take note of that. We will come back to it later.

3. Those who never step off the boat. Peter was the only one of all the disciples who stepped off that boat.

So here we see Jesus demonstrating living, active faith or great faith. The natural order of things did not matter to Him. Science would deny the possibility of any man walking on water. This was the design from the very beginning; if you step on water, you will sink. How did Jesus even know He could do that as a man? That is the power of faith. If you can dare to believe it, and not doubt, it can be done. But I can tell you it is much easier said than done. Although Jesus modeled it, we find it extremely difficult to look beyond what we see and know to even attempt to walk on water.

There was one man who dared. His name was Peter. He demonstrated little faith based on the simplest command I have seen in Scripture. Jesus said to him, "Come." In itself, this is a very conflicting predicament to be in. Will you believe God, or will you believe in the obvious circumstances that surround you? We are talking about water. No man has ever given thought to the possibility that one could walk on it like solid ground. But Peter saw Jesus standing on top of the water. If Jesus could, then surely he could too. The only challenge Peter had was to believe. That is what faith asks every time, "Will you believe?" Note that you exercise faith by acting on it. If Peter had believed, but not stepped off that boat, his faith would be a dead faith. Dead faith produces no fruit. Living faith produces more faith and more fruit. What practical sense is there to believe you can walk on water if you never do?

The third level of faith is dead faith. No one else on the boat acted on faith. James says faith without a corresponding action is DEAD. Faith provokes action. What does faith in action look like? I will show you when I talk about my struggle with fear. The bottom line is that faith sees beyond nature, time, space, matter, circumstances and most importantly, the reality of the physical world.

Every Christian falls into one of those three categories. We all need to move from dead and little faith to living and great faith. That is the level that pleases God and brings the realities of heaven to earth. That is the faith that releases what I call the Saint Mark 16:17-18 anointing:

"These signs will follow those who believe..."

Let's look at Peter a little bit more. Peter highlighted the one thing that deactivates our faith, and that is fear. Fear can cripple faith and render it fruitless. Fear and doubt are lovers and are hardly ever apart. For the Glorious Church to arise, we need to kick this couple out of the church, and out of our lives. We will talk about fear in the next chapter.

Prophetic Prayer

"Lord, give me spiritual wisdom and revelation so that I may know what is the hope of your calling, what is the wealth of your glorious inheritance in us, and what is the incomparable greatness of Your power towards us who believe." - Ephesians 1:17-19

Word

There is a way to get 100% results as Jesus did in healing and deliverance. We must develop an intimate relationship with Father, Son and Holy Spirit. He will direct us on what to do in all circumstances. If we do what the Father is doing in all situations, we will see 100% results.

Preach something that I can work with, says the Lord, preach messages that I can confirm with signs following, and I will work miracles among you. Jesus is the same yesterday, today and forever.

CHAPTER FIVE
Defeating Fear

Throughout the Scriptures, "Do not fear" and "Do not be afraid" and "Fear not" are repeated countless times. Every time there was a visitation by an Angel or the Lord, the first words spoken were, "Do not be afraid." Gideon heard it, so did Mary, Moses, and the Israelites. What is it about humanity that makes us so timid and afraid? Paul gave a glimpse into the reality of fear within the church when he said:

"For you did not receive a spirit that makes you a slave again to fear, but you received the Spirit of sonship..." - Romans 8:15

And again he addresses this is in I Timothy 1:7:

"For God did not give us a spirit of timidity (fear), but a spirit of power, of love and of self discipline."

Why did Paul need to keep reaffirming the church that we should not be motivated by fear?

A few years ago, gunmen invaded our church and made an attempt to get the keys to one of the vehicles parked just outside. Our pastor was there, and a few elders, one of which owned the vehicle. The young men with guns didn't care very much, and aggressively interrogated them to get the keys to the van but were only greeted with silence. Eventually, the young men left without the vehicle, and thankfully no one was hurt. There was an atmosphere of fear that blanketed the church for many weeks after that, and people have been reluctant to come out to night services even to this day.

In one of our other churches, gunmen chased a man down into the church and executed him at the altar in full view of children who had gathered for Vacation Bible School.

Do we have reasons for fear? Of course we do. We live in a fallen world, but fear should not hinder us from being obedient to God. As a matter of fact, God gives a direct and unquestionable command not to fear.

I don't think any of us lives a more dangerous life than King David did. He was constantly in battle, and had many enemies who wanted him dead, and he still lived to be a very old man. Listen to the words of this great man of faith:

"The Lord is with me; I will not be afraid. What can man do to me?" - Psalm 118:6

"Even though I walk through the valley of the shadow of death, I will fear no evil, for you are with me; your rod and your staff, they comfort me." - Psalm 23:4

A Glorious Church

"The Lord is my light and my salvation – whom shall I fear? The Lord is the stronghold of my life – of whom shall I be afraid?" - Psalm 27:1

This may sound like theology that contradicts with reality, but it doesn't. I am not just talking about Peter's inability to maintain faith while walking on top of the water; I am also talking about my own life. I will tell you my story in a little bit, but know that if I can overcome fear, anyone can.

Believe it or not, fear is simply the absence of faith. When fear steps in, faith leaves. The church is crippled by fear. Fear of witnessing to non-Christians. Fear of praying for the sick. Fear of death, sickness and pain. Fear is the reason our faith doesn't work. Fear is the reason we are afraid to move out of the comfort zones of tradition and routine and venture out into the waters. When Jesus was walking on water, the sea was rough, the wind was blowing hard, but everyone but Peter held on to the boat waiting for Jesus to come onboard. Jesus was not afraid.

Jesus is still standing on the water, and He gives an open invitation to the church, "Come." But we are crippled by fear. We dare not leave the boat. Jesus says, "I have not given you a spirit of fear, but of power, love and a sound mind, so come."

Do you want to know what is sad? We all know the Scriptures. In most cases, we can even quote them from memory:

If God be for me, who can be against me.

C. Orville McLeish

No weapons formed against us shall prosper, and every tongue that rise up against us shall fall.

God is my light and salvation. Whom shall I fear?

Greater is He who is in me than he that is in the world.

The enemy will always get permission to test what you believe. Untested faith is no faith at all. True faith has been tested and proven to be true. Heaven knows it's true, and the kingdom of darkness knows it's true.

I don't believe Jesus was talking to Peter alone. He told everyone on that boat to, "Come." It is an open invitation to all of us. Peter was the only one who did. I imagine everyone else must have been laughing and saying he was crazy. Nobody thought Jesus was crazy. They must have known by then that He could do anything, but He also demonstrated what we could do as well, if we believed. The problem then has always been a lack of active faith. I say active faith because I do believe that every born-again believer has been given a measure of faith (See Romans 12:3).

The boat was in the disciples' comfort zone; it was a kind of religion. Their trust, confidence, and faith were on that boat. They had no interest or desire to find out if they could walk on water like Jesus. However, Peter wanted to be where Jesus was, and Jesus was not on the boat. Jesus is looking for people today who are not afraid to walk on water. He's a

A Glorious Church

God of the impossible, not the possible. I put my faith in Him for what men say is impossible. That is my God. I like stepping off the boat. When Peter began to sink, the Lord reached out to him and saved him, so I am not worried about sinking. He has saved me many times, as I am determined to walk on water. But I wasn't always like that.

Growing up, I used to watch horror movies with my little sister (she's not so little anymore). I had no idea how those scenes would impact my life later on, but we are always breaking rules and doing stupid things with no thought for tomorrow.

Fear runs in my family line. My father lived eighty years in absolute fear. I don't know how far back in my family line it went, but this generation is as far as it goes for me. God knows my heart, and He knew just how to rid my life of what should not be there.

Let me share my personal testimony. I began to teach a series on spiritual warfare at church a few years ago. One week after the first lesson I ended up in the hospital for the first time in my life. I was at home alone. My sister and a few others had visited earlier and left. I got something to eat and sat to watch a Halloween episode of NCIS, slouched on the couch as usual, when I suddenly felt like I wasn't breathing. I panicked. I have never called for Jesus in my life like I did at that moment. I reached for the phone, called my wife at work. I didn't get her. I called my sister; they turned back. My wife then called me back, but in my mind, I thought they were too far to help me, so while hyperventilating, I went upstairs, got on some clothes, closed up the house and went outside. I thought if I fainted outside, it would be easy for someone just to scrape me up and carry me to wherever. My mind was filled to overflowing with fearful thoughts.

One of my neighbors was working on his car. He immediately took me to the nearest hospital where my wife met me. She had left work immediately. By this time, I wasn't feeling as 'dying' as before, just exhausted. My sister and company also joined us there. I saw a doctor, they ran some tests, did an ECG and then after a long interrogation, the doctor told me I had a panic attack. Up until that moment in my life, I had no idea what that was. I was discharged from the hospital the same night.

The next day, I called my doctor, and he gave me a prescription for stress pills, same pills they give to people suffering from depression. I knew depression. God had delivered me from it without medication many years ago during a very dark time in my life. Little did I know I was about to step into another very dark season of my life, wrestling almost daily with a spirit of fear. I had somehow developed what is known as anxiety, which is rooted in worry, stress and fear. This was all very new and uncomfortable for me, as that episode has repeated itself several times over the months that followed. I hated anxiety. I hated the medications even more. As a matter of fact, I was on my way to church one night and made a stop. While sitting in the car, I had a suicidal thought. That was scary. I didn't think I needed to take any medication that would cause me to think about suicide. So, I abandoned that remedy, trashed the pills and the prescription and dedicated my mental health to God as an act of faith. You would think faith in action would immediately liberate me, but it actually got excessively worse.

Anxiety is a mind-boggling condition. Imagine a state of mind that can replicate the real physical symptoms of a sickness, but you are really not sick. You are healthy but sick in a different way. What surprised me even more were the countless amounts of people who were suffering from this condition. I realize now that it is a device of the enemy to try and put sickness on you. If you believe you have the sickness associated with the symptoms long enough, the actual sickness will take root.

In my studies and seeking God I learnt a lot. God revealed a lot. We should learn from all our experiences, good and bad. Every experience you have in life has a valuable spiritual lesson attached to it. I learnt two very valuable lessons from my experience. Firstly, that initial day I ended up in the hospital, the enemy wanted me dead. I did not realize this until years later, but the doctors, hospitals or my neighbor did not save my life. I called out to Jesus, and He answered. There was nothing wrong with me by the time I got to the hospital. Secondly, I needed to make a choice.

A Christian cannot walk in faith and fear simultaneously. It is impossible. Doubt is the door that fear enters through, and fear is one of the devil's most effective weapons against Christians. It may just be his greatest weapon.

Let's look at the book of Genesis:

C. Orville McLeish

Now the serpent was more crafty than any of the wild animals the Lord God had made. He said to the woman, "Did God really say, 'You must not eat from any tree in the garden'? The woman said to the serpent, "We may eat fruit from the trees in the garden, but God did say, 'You must not eat fruit from the tree that is in the middle of the garden, and you must not touch it, or you will die.'" **"You will not certainly die***," the serpent said to the woman. "For God knows that when you eat from it your eyes will be opened, and you will be like God, knowing good and evil." When the woman saw that the fruit of the tree was good for food and pleasing to the eye, and also desirable for gaining wisdom, she took some and ate it. She also gave some to her husband, who was with her, and he ate it. Then the eyes of both of them were opened, and they realized they were naked; so they sewed fig leaves together and made coverings for themselves. Then the man and his wife heard the sound of the Lord God as he was walking in the garden in the cool of the day, and they hid from the Lord God among the trees of the garden. But the Lord God called to the man, "Where are you?" He answered, "I heard you in the garden, and I was* **afraid** *because I was naked; so I hid."* - Genesis 3:1-10

I love this story. It emphasizes a very important truth; the enemy has not changed his strategy. Man did not know fear until he doubted God's Word. Fear is rooted in unbelief, and unbelief is a sin.

I was afraid. Whenever there are any 'noises' in my body, I instantly started to feel fearful to the point that my body experiences some weird sensations. Through my experiences,

I realized that you can actually feel fear. Whenever I had a pain or some discomfort in my body, I immediately start thinking something is seriously wrong. A belly ache must be cancer. A headache must be a tumor. A chest ache must be a heart attack. I tell you, this is no way to live. The quality of your life is significantly reduced. I hated who I had become, but I had a choice. I understood the enemy's devices, so it was time to strike back. After all:

"Greater is He who is in me, than He that is in the world." - 1 John 4:4

Knowing was easy; believing it to the point of acting on it was a challenge. I have discovered that our greatest challenge in this Christian walk is not to acquire knowledge, but to exercise faith. The enemy tries to cast doubt on the Lord's Word, "Did God really say that he has healed you?" or "Did God really say he will provide your needs?" or "Did God really say he would always be there for you?" Subsequently, at the moment of doubt, a door is opened for fear to come in and take up residence. The devil wants you to believe that God is not greater and therein lies the challenge of overcoming fear.

If doubting God is the doorway for fear, then having faith keeps that door closed and fear has no entrance. This is easier said than done. This is a practical walk. What you know doesn't matter when you are in the field of trials. It is what you believe that carries weight.

C. Orville McLeish

In an act of faith, I stopped taking medications, stopped daydreaming about doctors and hospitals as my only hope to live, and started trusting God. That is when all hell broke loose. The enemy will not trouble you when you live in agreement with his words. When you stop, he comes against you like a flood. When I decided to put my faith in God, I got worst. I had several fevers, breathing issues, a whole bunch of noises in my body, fatigue, nausea, chronic cough, sometimes coughed up blood, and I felt like I was losing my mind, or dying. I knew there was no turning back for me.

The Lord gave me two really awesome revelations during these times. The first, *Faith is the substance of things hoped for, the evidence of things not seen.* I had to believe God for what I could not see. I was already healed, though the reality and gravity of my present reality said otherwise, I was already healed (See Isaiah 53:5; 1 Peter 2:24). It's hard to have faith when you are experiencing real symptoms. It's easier to put our faith in natural solutions than the sovereign, supernatural will of our loving Father. The second revelation I received was that if God, who is the greatest Ruler of the universe and Creator of all things, lives inside me, then what exactly do I fear? It means that anything that we fear has a lesser power than God. This revealed knowledge highlighted how severely deceived I was by the enemy. I did not really believe what God said, and I think that is the case for many of us. We doubt God and end up living our lives in fear.

The final analysis is this: I am a member of God's body and if He can't take care of His own body, then what hope do we truly have? So, God is my Plan A, and doctors, hospitals, and medication are plan B, if there is a plan B. I figure if plan A fails, then someone will execute plan B, or I go home to be with the Lord. Fear of death is a Christian's Pandora's Box, which is a major deception in itself as our hope and future are secured in Jesus Christ.

Fear has no place in you as a child of God, and if you stop to check the root of your fear, you will discover that somewhere you have been deceived into doubting what God says. Here is a nice revelation for you, the Holy Bible is God's written Word, and what He has written has already been established. If you take the written, established Word and write it on your heart, God will perform it.

Faith was a huge step for me. I once accepted poverty and the need to borrow money and go to doctors for every 'noise' and take medication, until God said to me one day, "At what point do you exercise your faith?" I think that was a relevant question. I believe in doctors and hospitals. I don't trust medications, but these should confirm what God is doing, or has done, not replace Him. Today when we have no money, we go take a loan. When we get sick, the doctor is our first thought and stop.

"Seek first the Kingdom of God, and His righteousness, and all these things will be added unto you." - St. Matthew 6:33

What would 'all these things' look like? Healing? Miracles? Finances? Mental health? Fear prevents us from accessing our inheritance in Christ, which is power, dominion, authority, health, forgiveness, wealth and a bright incomprehensible future. This contrasts with the reality of the church today, with Christians who are afraid of demons.

Learn to take steps of faith. Don't worry if you sink or look stupid. It is better to obey God than to please men. I am always attempting to walk on water. I believe that one day, I will not sink.

Fear stunted my growth as a Christian. I did not please God. I have made the choice that I would rather die pleasing God than live in fear and opposition to what He has said in His Word. God in His infinite wisdom allowed a sickness that is rooted in fear to force me to face fear head on and overcome it, so that my faith could be activated. I am a work in progress.

Faith is the only access we have to God, and I want what I read in the Bible. I don't want tradition and routine. Tradition and routine put people to sleep. When I go to church, I go to meet God. I go for an encounter with God. I don't go to be entertained, except by the presence of God.

We need to shut doubt's door in fear's face, so faith can once again heal the sick, cast out demons and raise the dead. The Name of Jesus spoken through faith will move mountains, dead will come back to life, sick will be healed, blind will see, deaf will hear, lame will walk, cancer must dry up, AIDS must dry up, headaches will be instantly gone: that is what the glorious Church looks like.

I have a lot of visions. I see morgues being emptied by the power of Jesus' Spirit. I see hospitals being emptied out as the afflicted are raised out of their beds by the power of God. All this is possible through His glorious Church, but first we must defeat fear.

Prophetic Word

You don't have to seek to get My attention, says the Lord, you had My attention long before you were conceived. Begin to declare and call forth what you want. There is a thin line between religion and relationship. It is not about waking up and getting the devotion out of the way so you can continue with your day. Religion brings guilt and condemnation. It is your perception of Me that drives your thoughts and emotions. I care about you. I care about what you think and do, and I want to be a part of your days, activities, choices and thoughts. Can you fathom that? I need you to divorce yourself from a religious mindset. I can only change people's lives through you in proportion to how much you change in your own life. Dig deeper. Come up higher. Leave the plains of fear and walk in the reality of My love. It is My perfect love that will defeat fear. It will not only defeat the fear in your heart, but it will establish you in My kingdom.

CHAPTER SIX
Our Natural Habitat

A while back, I was between sleep when I heard a voice say: *"I will re-establish My Church."* I have never had that experience before, hearing the audible voice of God, but I was also confused. In my mind, the church was already established, but the Lord began to reveal some truth to me concerning His will for the church. For years, I have been bothered by the noticeable difference between the church now and the church I read about in Acts and the Epistles, and that was what God was addressing.

If you are like me, you will be a little annoyed that we can pray for healing in Jesus name, and nothing happens. You will find it disheartening and frustrating that people around us keep dying of cancer, and all thirty-nine categories of sickness that Jesus bore in His body over two thousand years ago continues to afflict us unchallenged. The Prophet Isaiah decreed that: *"By His stripes we were healed."* Isaiah never met Jesus personally, yet he declared our healing in the present tense. According to this verse, we are (already) healed. Peter met Jesus, and he declared in 1 Peter 2:24:

"...by His wounds we have been healed."

C. Orville McLeish

These are the two clearest verses of Scripture in the Bible about our healing, and one is in the present tense and the other in the past tense. If this is true, then we don't have to be sick today or tomorrow.

There are many who accept as doctrine that healing is not for today, and while some may experience a miraculous recovery through natural means, most people die from acquired sickness with no hope of ever getting well. Where do you get your authority for doctrine? I have heard it said blatantly in church that not everyone is going to be healed. While in the natural, this may be true, in a spiritual sense we are telling God that His sacrifice was not sufficient. This is rather dangerous if you ask me. So let's really dissect these thoughts a bit. here is a thought to consider: *We are as much healed, as we are saved.* Jesus paid the full price for both. If healing is not for today, then neither is forgiveness. Would that explain why there is a culture of unforgiveness in the church? Jesus dealt with our sin, and He dealt with our infirmities. It is not His will for any to perish, and it is equally not His will for any to be sick. Sickness is not from God. If you read the gospels carefully, when Jesus healed the sick (all the sick) the Word says He delivered those oppressed by the devil.

I know you are ready to argue but let me ask you something: If you really, strongly believe that sickness is from God, then why do you go to doctors and take medications to try and get rid of the sickness? Aren't you in effect trying to get rid of God's will?

A Glorious Church

Sickness is not of God. God may allow the enemy to inflict us (as we see in Job), but it's really an occasion for Him to get the glory. Think about it. Job had lived before Jesus came to earth, so the price for healing was not yet paid. He wouldn't have that knowledge to declare the truth of Scripture, that by the stripes of Jesus he was healed. The devil afflicted him, but his affliction did not take his life. From Job, we can see that death is not the mandatory outcome for serious infirmity.

We can even take it one step further; Lazarus was dead for four days. Even if the enemy takes the life of one of God's precious jewels, the church has the right and power to bring them back. We have that right and that privilege, and we need to understand who we are in Christ. He has given us power over the enemy, over sickness, and even over death. It should be natural for us to cleanse the leper, heal the sick, cast out demons and raise the dead. That is our heritage and our inheritance. With that in mind, I think that our loving Father could easily give permission to the devil to inflict us as an opportunity to boast about His glorious Church as He has already paid the price, given us the keys to the kingdom, empowered us with His Spirit, and given us power, making us second in command to Him over all things. Imagine His disappointment. Because of who lives in us, everything that is subjected to Jesus is also subjected to us, but this can only be appropriated through faith. We suffer then because of our ignorance and our reluctance to assume our position in Christ. God says:

"My people perish for lack of knowledge."

C. Orville McLeish

We really are perishing. We are actually sick, fearful, tormented and dying and there is no power on earth to change this because the church is caught up in activities, and maintaining a religious front while cowering and crippled by fear in a little corner of the world.

I believe that God is addressing this problem in the church today. He is re-establishing *His* Church on the foundation of power and authority, just as the early church. This is a good thing, Amen. So one of my responsibilities as a minister is to teach and preach the Kingdom of God. The glory or presence of God is key to our existence as a church.

With all that I do, I always start at the beginning. The beginning teaches us the truth about our existence and our purpose. In the beginning, God created the sea, and then He made the fish. Why didn't He create the fish first? Because the body of water called the sea is the fish's natural habitat. So first He created the environment that the fish can live and grow in, and then He made the fish. What happens to a fish when it is removed from the sea?

God then created the earth, then flowers and trees, then the animals. He created a natural habitat for animals before putting them there. Likewise, He created the air, then the birds. For each living creature, God first created the natural habitat for it to survive.

The natural habitat for man is the *Glory*, the very presence of God. One preacher describes the glory as *the atmosphere of heaven*. That atmosphere left the earth after man sinned, came back to earth for short periods of time throughout the Old Testament, but came fully in the person of Jesus Christ and imparted to us, and has never left. According to Isaiah 43:7:

*"God created us for His **glory**."*

The Bible says that when Adam and Eve sinned, they heard the voice of the Lord coming, and they went and:

"hid from the presence of the Lord God." - Genesis 3:8

Adam and Eve hid from what? The PRESENCE of the Lord God. Throughout history, God has always desired to tabernacle with men. We see this with the Ark of the Covenant, and also the Tabernacle where the holy of holies was located. According to the Scripture, where these were, the presence of God rested on the earth.

Jesus came. Through Him, we became the house of God. We are the tabernacle where the glory of God dwells; we are carriers of His presence. God no longer dwells in houses made by human hands. He lives in the very vessels that He created with His own hands; our body is a house that God built for Himself. This means wherever we are out there in the world, the presence of God should be there with us. If the glory of God is the atmosphere of heaven, then the kingdom of darkness should know when we walk into a room.

The problem is that too many of us live outside the presence of God. Like Adam and Eve, it is still possible for us to hide from God's presence right there in church while sitting in the pews or the choir, and while amongst the congregation. We hide from God's presence when we choose to embrace sin. *We need to stop hiding and begin to exist in the Glory of God, which is our natural habitat.*

The House of God

Genesis 28 tells us that Isaac sent Jacob away from his homeland to Padanaram to choose a wife. On his way, Jacob stopped at a certain place to sleep for the night. He used a stone as a pillow and fell asleep in that place. He then had a vision. He saw a ladder set up on the earth, and the top of it reached heaven, and there were angels ascending and descending on it. When Jacob woke up, he said in verses 16 & 17:

"Surely the Lord is in this place; and I knew it not. And he was afraid, and said, how dreadful is this place! This is none other but the house of God, and this is the gate of heaven."

We can be where the presence and glory of God are manifested and not even perceive it. The Bible says, we have all sinned and fallen short of the glory of God. We were made to live in the presence of God. We must begin to see ourselves as the house of God, and not doubt. Unbelief is a sin that can separate us from the presence of God that indwells us. Romans 14:23 says:

"...whatever does not proceed from faith is sin."

The sin that separates the church from the glory is a lack of absolute faith in God's Word.

Just as water is the natural habitat for fish, and earth for plants, our natural habitat is the presence of God or in His glory. We have fallen short of the glory of God. The problem is that too many of us live outside the presence of God. He has given us access to the holy of holies, but we are more comfortable in the outer courts. That is why we are so cold, lukewarm, dry or dead. We can't worship. We can't pray. We can't relate to God because we exist outside His presence. What happens to a fish when removed from the water? What happens to a plant when removed from the earth? What happens to us when we are removed from the presence of almighty God? It is not necessarily a physical death, but our soul loses its life and vitality. God absolutely hates it when we call him a liar. If He says something in His Word, that is exactly what He means, and we need to appropriate those truths. After all:

"God is not human, that he should lie, not a human being, that he should change his mind. Does he speak and then not act? Does he promise and not fulfill?" - Numbers 23:19 – NIV

We live in an age and time when a lot of 'dead' people come to church. I used to be one of them. We have reduced Christianity to a dead religion built on traditions and rituals and the absence of God's glory. I prophesy to every dead bone and soul reading this book that *you shall live.* Rise up and take your inheritance. As a man, I have been given authority and dominion over this earth.

The Lord gave me a vision that I really liked. There was a very large gathering at a very large church, and a coffin was brought to the stage. It was a funeral, but what was dead and in the coffin was not a man, but religion. We had a nice burial service for Religion. The presence of God needs to return to our churches, but there are things that must go for this to be realized.

In God's presence there is the fullness of joy, and at His right hand pleasures forevermore. If you are not experiencing joy in the things of God, or if you are constantly depressed and sad, you are not in God's presence. We need to live in the glory of God.

"For in him we live and move and exist." - Acts 17:28

People tend to respond to the glory of God in different ways. Let's look at some examples:

1. Isaiah experienced God's presence filling a room that he was in. He fell down and cried: *"Woe is me! For I am undone; because I am a man of unclean lips, and I dwell in the midst of a people of unclean lips: for mine eyes have seen the King, the LORD of hosts."*

2. Moses experienced the glory of God and the Bible says his face "shone." Every time he entered into the presence of God and came out, they had to put a veil

A Glorious Church

over his face just to be able to look at him.

3. Moses understood the presence of God. He had a very interesting conversation with God in Exodus 33:12-18:

Moses said to the Lord, "You have been telling me, 'Lead these people,' but you have not let me know whom you will send with me. You have said, 'I know you by name and you have found favor with me.' If you are pleased with me, teach me your ways so I may know you and continue to find favor with you. Remember that this nation is your people." The Lord replied, "My Presence will go with you, and I will give you rest." *Then Moses said to him, "If your Presence does not go with us, do not send us up from here. How will anyone know that you are pleased with me and with your people unless you go with us? What else will distinguish me and your people from all the other people on the face of the earth?" And the Lord* said to Moses, "I will do the very thing you have asked, because I am pleased with you and I know you by name." *Then Moses said, "Now show me your glory."* (NIV).

- Peter was surrounded by God's glory. Scripture says people wanted to come in contact with his very shadow, I believe, with the hope of being healed.

- Paul and Silas praised until the glory of God fell. What happened? Freedom, not just for them, but for all the prisoners.

We cannot continue to exist outside of God's presence. We need His glory. We need to dwell in His atmosphere, if we are to walk as His true church. We cannot be content with just existing outside this atmosphere. We can live in and experience God's glory.

The first time I experienced the tangible presence of God was not in church. I was at school, and the teacher was teaching on the Church of God of Prophecy. There was a timely raising of a specific song that totally changed the atmosphere. I have never had that experience before. We were so engrossed in the presence that we even lost the appetite for food, and that has never happened to me.

Where the name of God is genuinely praised, His glory will reside. Where men and women worship in spirit and truth is where the glory of God will descend. It's like a cloud we often refer to as the *Shekinah Glory.* It's a tangible manifestation of God's nature among men. You can perceive His glory with your five senses. It is manufactured by praise. The Holy Spirit gathers the praise of genuine worshippers and builds this cloud similar to clouds of rain. When it is full, the rains come. When the glory of God fills a place, everything changes. No demon can stay where the glory manifests. No sickness can stay where the glory manifests. The spirit of poverty and lack cannot stand where the glory of God manifest.

The Word is good, but the Word only tells us what we need to do, and what we will get. Tradition has its place, but it does not change the hearts and minds of men. It cannot root out demons nor heal sicknesses. Christianity is just another dead religion without the glory of God.

We are not short of knowledge, but we lack experience. That is why our testimonies are fabricated or borrowed. I know what God did over two thousand years ago. It's historical fact. What I want to know is what God is doing today! We gain nothing by existing outside the presence of God. Literally, outside of God's glory, we should feel like a fish out of the water, like a plant pulled up out of the ground and laid aside. We need to be in the presence of God. We need to be surrounded by His glory.

Isaiah prophesied in Isaiah 40:5:

"And the glory of the Lord shall be revealed, and all flesh shall see it together; for the mouth of the Lord has spoken it."

I have read this so many times that I am starting to believe it to be true that *God wants to reveal Himself to us, more than we want Him to.*

We need to stop talking about the glory and step into it. We do that through: Repentance, Faith, Praise and Worship.

The glorious Church must take up permanent residence in the glory of God. Otherwise, we are just another powerless religion, having a form of Godliness, but denying the power thereof.

C. Orville McLeish

Prophetic Word

Eye hath not seen, nor ear heard, neither have entered into the heart of man, the things which God hath prepared for them that love him. There is a mystery that hath been hidden from ages and from generations, but now is made manifest to you, to make known what is the riches of the glory of this mystery among you, which is Christ in you, the hope of glory. To you, it is given to know the mystery of the Kingdom of God. You are a king and priest in the earth, and all the mysteries of the kingdom are made available for you to seek out. If you seek, you will find. Ask and it will be given. Knock and the door will be open to you.

CHAPTER SEVEN
Suffering in Silence

Breaking silence was a very tough lesson for me because I am a quiet person by nature. I was so consumed by my own silence that when I met my wife, and we started talking for hours on the phone, my conscience literally condemned me. I have never talked so much in my life, and my prayer life as a Christian had been severely hampered by my reluctance to speak. I had to change, or my life would never change. There is something remarkable about the spoken word that I want to bring out in this chapter. If we can understand this concept, we can experience levels of freedom we never thought possible.

Very often we don't suffer in silence; we suffer because we are silent. Our breakthrough is divinely etched into the words that leave our mouths, which is why we are so adequately cautioned on many occasions not to use our tongue loosely.

Most Christians don't have a clue that what they experience is influenced by what they say. To establish this biblical truth, let us examine one member of our body, the tongue.

In James 3:1-12, we see several attributes of the tongue that we must never overlook:

- The tongue is a small part of the body. The tongue makes great boast.

- The tongue is a fire (not like a fire). The tongue corrupts the whole body.

- The tongue sets the whole course of one's life on fire. The tongue cannot be tamed by human beings.

The entire course of our lives is affected by what we say. Among other uses, this small member of our body gives us the ability to speak and what we say matters! Proverbs 18:21 reads:

"The tongue has the power of life and death…" (The wisest man who ever lived spoke those words), "…and those who love it will eat its fruit." The tongue has power! (emphasis mine).

For us to fully understand the gravity of what we say, it is necessary that we go back to the first book of the Bible. Genesis 1:26 tells us:

"Then God said, 'Let us make mankind in our image, in our likeness, so that they may rule over the fish in the sea and the birds in the sky, over the livestock and all the wild animals, and over all the creatures that move along the ground.'"

We were created like God. What does it mean to be like God? David says: "…You are gods, and all of you are children of the Most High." (Psalm 82:6). This is a powerful statement to make about human beings. The suggestion here is that there is a similarity in scope and design, not a perfect replica, but a limited by-version of who God is.

Who is God, and what is He like? Genesis 1:1 says: *"In the beginning God..."* (no explanation for God's beginning or existence, but He just is).

There really is no other way to introduce God. He has always been, always is and always will be. We are the ones with a beginning, and if we try to quantify God within the limitations of such reasoning, we are going to encounter confusion and misconception.

For years, I tried to figure out where God had come from. If man has been in existence for 6,000 (assumed) years, then how many years has God been in existence? How did He come into existence? These questions reveal human limitations. If you carefully examine the book of Job, you will see a man asking similar questions only to be greeted with questions for which he had no answers.

God cannot be understood within the framework of time because time was created, and time was created for man. Real time is eternity, a reality of which we will know at our death or translation (like Enoch and Elijah). I believe time was created encapsulated inside eternity, like a small cocoon, which means time has a beginning and an end. Human beings exist in time in the flesh, but originated outside of time, especially those who are born again (born from above).

C. Orville McLeish

In the beginning, God created. How did God create? He spoke worlds into being. He said, *"Let there be..."* and there was. If we are like God, especially now as a redeemed community of people (meaning we have been restored to God through Jesus Christ as Adam was before he sinned), then we are once again restored to the image and likeness of God. The possibility exists then, that if He can speak things into existence, then so can we.

This thought is clearer when we read Genesis 2:19-20:

"Now the Lord had formed out of the ground all the wild animals and all the birds in the sky. He brought them to the man to see what he would name them; and whatever the man called each living creature, that was its name. So the man gave names to all the livestock, the birds in the sky and all the wild animals..."

Whatever the man CALLED each living creature, that was its name. So Adam called that nice, fluffy feline 'CAT' and that creature is named Cat to this day. Adam spoke it, and it was so.

When God made man, He put power in our tongue so we can speak things into being, just like He can. I know this may be hard to believe because our minds may be warped by the lies of the deceiver. The closer I get to God, the more I realize how many lies I have believed. Beloved, it is easy to be convinced of a lie or a half truth. If we are going to be the Church that God designed us to be, we must be willing to unlearn and relearn. It is a painful but necessary process.

Jesus came on the scene as a perfect example of a redeemed man. He died so we can be just like Him in this world. One of the lies of the enemy is that Jesus was God, and it is impossible for us to be like Him. That is half true. Jesus is God, but He put off His divinity and walked this earth as a complete, fully manifested Man. What He did, we can do and even more. He said it. Jesus said, *"Greater works we will do..."* and I believe we are living in the era of greater works!

In some places in the world, we are seeing limbs growing back and damaged organs being replaced in the bodies of God's people. There have been numerous supernatural healings from deadly diseases and testimonies of fat supernaturally melting off people in a matter of seconds.

Jesus says that if we believe, then all things are possible. It amazes me that we put the same limitations on God that we put on ourselves. In essence, we really don't believe that God can do what we cannot.

Mark 11:12-24 says:

"And on the morrow, when they came from Bethany, he was hungry: And seeing a fig tree afar off having leaves, he came, if haply he might find anything thereon: and when he came to it, he found nothing but leaves; for the time of figs was not yet. And Jesus answered and said unto it, No man eat fruit of thee hereafter for ever. And his disciples heard it. And they come to Jerusalem: and Jesus went into the temple, and began to cast out them that sold and bought in the temple, and overthrew the

tables of the moneychangers, and the seats of them that sold doves; and would not suffer that any man should carry any vessel through the temple. And he taught, saying unto them, Is it not written, My house shall be called of all nations the house of prayer? but ye have made it a den of thieves. And the scribes and chief priests heard it and sought how they might destroy him: for they feared him because all the people were astonished at his doctrine. And when even was come, he went out of the city. And in the morning, as they passed by, they saw the fig tree dried up from the roots. And Peter calling to remembrance saith unto him, Master, behold the fig tree which thou cursedst is withered away. And Jesus answering saith unto them, Have faith in God. For verily I say unto you, That whosoever shall say unto this mountain, Be thou removed, and be thou cast into the sea; and shall not doubt in his heart, but shall believe that those things which he saith shall come to pass; he shall have whatsoever he saith. Therefore I say unto you, What things soever ye desire, when ye pray, believe that ye receive them, and ye shall have them."

Jesus used this opportunity to teach us a very valuable lesson on the power of faith. He said that no one would ever eat fruit from the tree again. His disciples heard Him say it. By the next morning, the tree had withered from the roots. It died. Jesus said:

"If you have faith you can SAY to the mountain move and if you have no doubt, but believe what you SAY will happen, it will be done."

We can argue all we want as to whether Jesus was implying an actual mountain, or was speaking figuratively, but either way, the church has not been moving any kinds of mountains in a while.

The Scripture says:

"When you ASK for anything in prayer, believe you have received it, and it's yours."

Now let us be honest. When is the last time you prayed a specific prayer, and had the joy of seeing it answered?

The course of our lives is determined by the words that we speak by faith. What we say matters. We like to read about all the great powerful acts that came to pass from spoken words, but in reality, we might feel foolish speaking to trees and mountains. Observers might draw conclusions about our sanity. Maybe that is the reason we don't say what God is saying: we are too busy being mindful of how it looks and feels.

To highlight the power of our words, let's look at three specific Scriptures:

"A fool's lips enter into contention, and his mouth calleth for strokes. A fool's mouth is his destruction, and his lips are the snare of his soul. The words of a talebearer are as wounds, and they go down into the innermost parts of the belly." - Proverbs 18:6-8

C. Orville McLeish

"The words of a talebearer are as wounds, and they go down into the innermost parts of the belly." - Proverbs 26:22

"My soul is among lions: and I lie even among them that are set on fire, even the sons of men, whose teeth are spears and arrows, and their tongue a sharp sword." - Psalm 57:4

The enemy has desensitized us to the power and use of our tongues. He has silenced us, and he has been doing it from a very young age. Recall the saying: "Sticks and stones may break my bones, but words can never hurt me." In actuality, words can give life or words can kill.

The world uses guns and knives to take life. The church uses its tongue. The enemy knows the power embedded in your tongue. Life then becomes a matter of perspective, for though the Bible tells us succinctly that we wrestle not against flesh and blood, the enemy deceives us into thinking we are each other's enemies. I find it amazing what we release in the atmosphere about each other, what we speak behind closed doors. I know the power of words and have spent a great deal of my life fighting word curses.

Recently, I kept having a sticking feeling in my head. I know the Lord saw my concern, and this was His response, "That is what it feels like in the natural when someone is talking about you behind your back." Do we hate those who do that? No! We pray for them and bless them. We forgive them because they do not know what they are doing. Jesus said on the cross, "Forgive them, for they don't know what they are doing."

A Glorious Church

Hebrews 4:12 says:

"For the Word of God is quick, and powerful, and sharper than any two edged sword, piercing even to the dividing asunder of soul and spirit, and of the joints and marrow, and is a discerner of the thoughts and intents of the heart."

When we take the Word of God, and put it on our tongues and release it, things happen. I want you to note that a two-edged sword has two sides, and both sides are sharp, so it cuts both ways. If you are one of those misbehaving Christians like me who have watched Spartacus (I don't watch it anymore), you know that one easy swipe can take off a man's foot or head. The Word of God is sharper than that.

But the opposite is also true. Negative words and gossip are also like spears, darts and swords that can go deep into your soul and affect every area of your life.

There is a very famous saying, "If you have nothing good to say, do not say anything at all." Interestingly, I don't know which is worse: to speak negatively, or not to speak at all. Silence may not be the answer. We need to change what we say.

When Jesus was tempted by the devil after forty days of fasting, Jesus responded to each temptation with: *"It is written..."* Understand that it was not the written word that had the power, but the written word SPOKEN.

Ephesians 6:16 says:

"....in addition to the whole armor, take up the shield of faith, with which you can extinguish (or block) all the flaming arrows of the evil one."

"Flaming arrows" can be words thrown at you by others. Faith is important in our Christian walk. To define faith, I would say it is a confident assurance in God and His promises, and in who we are in God. Most of us have never seen God. We can barely trust each other who we can see, much less put our full confidence in one we cannot see.

Let's engage our imaginations for just for a bit. We all face challenges, and most of us experience difficulties that are beyond our control. The easy Biblical answer is to speak to your mountains and watch them move. Reality sometimes teaches us differently. So, like the children of Israel, we are standing on a ridge. In front is the vast Red Sea, and behind the enemy is drawing closer to take our lives. They literally have blood in their eyes, because your God took their first-born sons. They are upset.

Now think about all you know and believe about God and see if you can ascertain what your trend of thought would be at that moment. You have never seen a sea part so that option is not even remotely in your subconscious mind. What are you feeling? What are you thinking? Remember, God says that you can do all things. In that moment, what would 'all things' look like to you? I use this example to highlight the challenge we face as a church who believes God. Many of us would probably just fold up and let whatever happens just happen. That is not quite the response God would expect from one of His sons or daughters.

The truth is, God has made it quite simple for us. He took our infirmities, sicknesses, pains, sorrows, burdens and lack. If He took it, then it no longer belongs to us. If we refuse to accept sickness, we are not lying. Sickness is not ours because Jesus carried it.

Our words then cannot be influenced by our present reality, but by the truth of God's Word. We need to speak and declare until what we say manifests in the natural world.

If the enemy tries to convince you that you are ugly, respond with, "It is written that I am fearfully and wonderfully made." There is no need to quote which chapter and verse it is. Jesus did not do that, so it is not a requirement.

If the enemy tries to convince you that you are worthless and good for nothing, "It is written that I am co-heir with Christ to inherit the Kingdom of God."

If the enemy puts sickness on you, "It is written that by His stripes I am healed. God wishes above all things that I prosper, and be in good health, even as my soul prospers."

If the enemy tries to convince you that you are poor, and you will always be in lack and struggling, "It is written that Jesus became poor that I might become rich."

There are young people especially who have been convinced that they are nothing, just an accident from a random act of pleasure, but: "It is written that I am the righteousness of God, through Jesus Christ, and God knew me before I was in my mother's womb."

We need to speak the Word of God over our lives, our minds, our children, our families and our nations. We need to stop perpetuating the lies of the enemy. There is no truth in the enemy, but he knows that our lives are the sum totals of what we believe. What happens when you believe and speak the lies? What happens when we speak the truth?

You can tell how much of the Word dwells in Christians by what they say when they speak. There is no middle ground in our existence. We either believe the truth, or we believe a lie. If we are to be the church, our minds must be renewed with the truth of God's Word.

In my own Christian life growing up, I used to seek for more of God without committing to the study of His Word. I never fully understood why He withheld so much, until recently. The Bible is true, and there is nothing else you can measure a revelation or thought against to know if it is true.

One of the struggles I had was how farfetched the Word of God seemed in my own life. Understanding that it was always His will for me to be healed and not sick, rich and not poor, strong and not weak, was a big pill to swallow, but it exposed the enemy's lies in my own mind. As the strongholds in my life started crumbling, I was uncomfortable. I felt dizzy, nauseous most of the time, weak and fatigued, and there were many issues in my body as my mind went through an overhaul. Many Christians choose not to go through the process because of the discomfort. I purposed in my mind that if I was to be pure gold, I must subscribe to the fire.

My words changed when I stopped agreeing with the enemy, and conversations with some people became hard, so my friends also changed.

If you are tired of suffering, and you desire the authentic power of God to operate in your life leading you to ultimate victory, there is a price to pay.

One of the greatest revelations I have received is that we must *conquer to possess*. The land of healing, miracles, signs, wonders, liberty, deliverance and prosperity is already ours, but we must possess it. We must displace those who have occupied the lands due to our neglect and ignorance to truth, and possess the lands that Jesus purchased with His blood. Some of us need to stop singing, "I want to go to heaven and rest," and get busy establishing the kingdom of God on earth. All our gifts and talents were given to us for a reason. Even creating wealth is not so much about the money but bringing ideas from heaven and establishing them on the earth.

God has put His Word in your mouth, so release it. You no

longer need to suffer in silence. You are a child of the truth, so stop speaking lies. Get these thoughts out of your mind:

- *I am not going to make it*
- *I am a failure*
- *Things will never get better*
- *I am worthless*
- *God hates me*
- *I am a sufferer*
- *I will always be sick*
- *I will never get anywhere in life*
- *I am nobody*
- *My life is insignificant*
- *I might as well be dead*

Imagine having all these darts and swords lodged in our spirits. No wonder we feel so depleted and defeated. God has led me into literally pulling these swords out of my own spirit. He wants to set us free from the words that have been spoken over our lives by ourselves and others.

John 1:1-3 says:

"In the beginning was the Word, and the Word was with God, and the Word was God. He was with God in the beginning. Through Him all things were made; without him nothing was made that has been made."

Jesus Christ is the Word of God. Jesus Christ lives in us

through the Holy Spirit.

1 Corinthians 6:19 says:

"Do you not know that your bodies are temples of the Holy Spirit, who is in you, whom you have received from God? You are not your own."

So the WORD that created all things lives in us. That is why Jesus said that by faith we can speak it, and it will be done. If you find yourself struggling, or suffering consistently, if you are addicted to sin and can't be free, if you are unemployed but just can't seem to find work, if you are sick and can't seem to get well, if you are broke no matter how much money you make, you may be saying the wrong things.

The power is in your own tongue to change the course of your life and to set at liberty those who are oppressed. Use it to the glory of God.

As I write, my processing continues. I have been having a feeling of food stuck in my throat for months. It is really uncomfortable, in addition to other discomforts I have been experiencing in my body. I believe the Lord is teaching me to discern the spiritual world. Everything that happens in the natural realm has its origins in the spiritual realm (the real world). Most Christians are not living this reality. Anyway, I kept thinking about this lump in my throat until I heard the voice of the Lord say, "Have you spoken to the condition?" Right away I commanded the lump to go and guess what? It did. We have to be careful that we don't give people solutions that we ourselves do not practice.

Prophetic Word

I created you to be a speaking spirit, so speak. Don't be silent when everything is going wrong in your life. As the Word leaving my mouth is spirit and life, so is yours because my Spirit dwells in you. I am calling you to a higher place, to a greater experience in my presence. Every time you open your mouth, you must agree with heaven. There are no such things as wasted words. As you speak you build, things begin to shift, move, and change. Don't judge reality by what you see. *Create reality by what you speak.* I have given you everything you need to live the abundant life. Conquer to possess. You are a warrior. You are a king. You are a priest. You are a soldier. You have My armor, My authority, and dominion. You must conquer and possess. The land is yours.

CHAPTER EIGHT
God Still Speaks

My desperation to hear God grew to exponential levels in less than three years of seeking Him. I was desperate, but God knew that before I could successfully walk in His glory, and hear His voice, I needed His Word in my heart so I would not be deceived. One thing I have learnt about the enemy is that when he counterfeits something Godly, it looks almost exactly like the original. Deceiving us is easy if we do not know the Word of God. For instance, I grew up in church hearing and believing that God does not need us. Now I know that if that were true, He would not have bothered coming to earth to save man. Why would He do that, if He had no interest in us or use for us? We were created by Him and for Him. If the church is the bride of Christ, as some teach, which loving husband would ever make such a statement that he does not need his bride?

I have been a lifelong member of The Church of God of Prophecy in Jamaica. For the most part, I was an avid observer. I was literally behind the scenes, and somehow from what I heard and what I saw, I knew there was something *off* with the church. This was gravely highlighted when I started to read the gospels. I could not figure out why today's church did not resemble the church in the Bible.

C. Orville McLeish

I am happy for my church's strong belief in Pneumatology, which is the study of the Holy Spirit. We believe He is essential to the life of every believer. Without Him, we lose our connection to God and the spiritual realm.

Holy Spirit plays multiple roles in our lives:

- He applies the work of the cross.
- He is the power of resurrection.
- He is the bringer of gifts from God.
- He helps us pray.
- He guides (lead us into all truth).
- He protects.
- He illuminates Scripture.
- He's multilingual (speaks many languages).

We need Holy Spirit in all facets of our existence. What I want to focus on now is His voice in this world. It would be remiss of us to think that God stopped speaking at Revelation 22:21. God had a lot to say before Genesis, and He will have a lot to say for all eternity.

Jesus demonstrated something that is vital to a Christian's life. He mentions that He only did what He *saw* His Father do. *Saw* denotes seeing with the eyes. But it was Jesus who also said:

"No one has seen the Father, but He who came from the Father."

Jesus, as a man, could see the Father. His ability to know what the Father was doing was in His ability to hear and see. In the spiritual realm, you can also see by hearing.

I have read a lot of books by men and women who were walking in the supernatural, but none of them had seen 100% result in healing and miracles as Jesus and the early church saw. In consideration, the Lord gave me the answer. If we are to see 100%, we need to hear what the Father wants to do in each situation.

Now, it is never God's will for us to be sick, meaning He desires for us to be healed. Why else would He carry our sicknesses and diseases? The question then becomes, how does God want to heal in a particular situation? This question took me a good while to process, and even as I write, I am still learning. Nothing happens in the physical realm without first happening in the spiritual realm. When sickness hits your body, it has its origins in the spiritual realm. It makes sense that Paul said:

"Our battle is not against flesh and blood, but against principalities, powers..."

If we fight our battles in the spiritual realm, we walk in greater victories in the physical realm. To fight effectively, we need to be able to hear.

God has never been silent, but in many instances, men have stopped listening. There is a very deep revelation found in the story of Adam's fall in Genesis 3. After the first man sinned,

C. Orville McLeish

Genesis 3:8 says:

> *"Then the man and his wife **heard** the sound of the Lord God as he was walking in the garden in the cool of the day, and they hid from the Lord God among the trees of the Garden."*

We still see this response to God by sinful men. We hear God, but we seek to hide from Him. I find it interesting that even with the fall, men still had the ability to hear God. It makes sense when you really think about it. How will a man come to God, if he is unable to hear God? If God calls us, then surely He speaks to us.

The relationship between God and man was restored through the death and resurrection of Jesus. This suggests that whoever we were before sin, is who we can be today. Interestingly, Jesus came down in the cool of the day to commune with man before the fall. We can have that same relationship today.

One of the problems we have as Christians is that we don't listen to what God has to say. Most Christians are unable to identify His voice. Most Christians don't know His voice. We need to know the voice of our Shepherd. How else will we walk in obedience?

John 10:27 says:

> *"My sheep listen to my voice; I know them, and they follow me."*

A Glorious Church

The Shepherd speaks to different people in different ways. For me, He uses images. I see myself doing something, and I obey by doing what I saw. I believe that in acting out those images, heaven literally meets earth, and they become one. It felt foolish at first, and still does sometimes, but it is worth getting used to. It is not always easy to obey God, and it will sometimes look peculiar to observers. If you are overly concerned about what people think, you run the risk of not obeying God when He speaks. He has a tendency to make some very unusual requests.

I once saw myself in a classroom with a particular teacher discussing a particular subject. I had forgotten about that vision until I caught up to that time in my future. I was sitting in class with a particular teacher, talking about a particular thing. I had a déjà vu moment, and while I was experiencing that moment for the first time, in essence, it had already happened.

Interesting, it makes sense when the Bible says Jesus was crucified before the foundation of the earth (See Revelation 13:8). Nothing happens in the physical realm without first originating in the spirit realm.

There are times when I am going on a long trip, and I see myself laying hands on the car and praying for it. I do just that, and the journey is safe and incident free. To onlookers, think how strange it must look in our culture for me to rest my hands on the hood of a car, bow my head, close my eyes and pray. That is the reality of who we are in this world.

C. Orville McLeish

How does God, our Shepherd, communicate with you? Through dreams? The still small voice of the Holy Spirit? Through visions? Through others?

Please note that God is a Spirit, so He communicates through the Spirit. It is not wise for us to expect to hear God audibly, even though a few people have had that experience and we can too. God is not obligated to speak audibly to anyone, but He is God, and He can if he desires. I spent most of my Christian life expecting Him to act and speak dramatically and could never fathom why He refused me that experience. I know better now.

God speaks through His Holy Spirit to our soul. His voice may sound exactly the same as our inward voice. As a matter of fact, all the voices in our heads sound familiar. To know who is speaking, we need to examine fruit and content. The only standard on earth for truth and righteousness is the Word of God. God will never say anything that cannot be confirmed by His Word. He will never contradict Himself.

God speaks to us through the Holy Spirit. There are no other means of communication between God and us, and He will speak to us about everything. In my experience that when I take on the simplest of tasks without prior knowledge, if I stop long enough and quiet my soul, God will tell me what to do. I have solved many mysteries with God's help. Most recently I was installing a toilet seat, which was almost an impossible task because it was fixed against the wall with not enough room for my hand to get around it. In one quiet moment, Holy Spirit told me exactly what to do, and it worked perfectly. Jesus made a deep statement about the Holy Spirit:

John 16:13 *says:*

"But when he, the Spirit of truth, comes, he will guide you into all the truth. He will not speak on his own; he will speak only what he hears, and he will tell you what is yet to come."

The Holy Spirit has a mind of His own, suggesting that He could speak His own mind, but Jesus said that He would only speak what He hears. I believe there is far more to God than Genesis to Revelation, but what is contained within those pages, combined with time to read and study, is all we need for life and Godliness (See 2 Peter 1:3). There are many mysteries to unfold, depths to discover, and heights to attain. God created a framework for our existence where, despite the attempts of the kingdom of darkness, we can know God. The world, the flesh and the devil are louder than God today, but through His Word and Spirit, we can know Him. We can know what He is saying, and what He wants us to do.

"Jesus only DID what He saw the Father doing." - John 5:19

"The Holy Spirit only SAYS what He hears the Father saying."
- John 16:13

Jesus is God's action towards us. The Word made flesh. The Holy Spirit is God's means of speaking to us. The Holy Spirit is our ONLY connection to God, and He lives in us. He is the same Spirit who moved upon the face of the earth in Genesis 1. He is the same Spirit who rose Jesus from the dead after three days. He is the same Spirit who empowers normal people like you and me to do great and supernatural things.

So let's be practical about this. There are at least three voices in your head:

- Your own voice.
- The voice of the Spirit of Truth.
- The voice of the father of lies.

Your voice is connected to your fallen nature and can easily be influenced by the father of lies or your emotions. Your voice supports laziness, carnality and fleshly desires and cravings. Your voice says sleep some more, eat some more, do not exercise, etc. Your voice opposes the voice of the Spirit of Truth.

The Spirit of Truth will tell you to fast, pray, exercise, eat right, lay hands on the sick, speak a word of comfort to your brother or sister, give money to that poor man, give more offering, sow your tithes, hug your brother or sister, love your enemies, etc., all supported by Scripture. All other voices seek to oppose or try to establish a subculture that looks like the truth but is a perverted version of it.

Galatians 5:17 says:

"For the flesh desires what is contrary to the Spirit, and the Spirit what is contrary to the flesh. They are in conflict with each other, so that you are not to do whatever you want."

The Spirit of Truth can oppose our thoughts or those of the father of lies because, at all times, the Spirit knows our every thought. The Spirit of Truth can neutralize that inappropriate thought we may have towards a sister or brother. We also must remember to be mindful of what we say.

The Holy Spirit knows your thoughts. He will sometimes assume a personal position with us and speak accordingly:

- "I need to pray."
- "I should fast."
- "I should take better care of God's temple."

We need to know the voice of our Shepherd, and we need to be willing to obey when He speaks to us.

1 Corinthians 2:14 says:

"The person without the Spirit does not accept the things that come from the Spirit of God but considers them foolishness, and cannot understand them because they are discerned only through the Spirit."

C. Orville McLeish

Without the Holy Spirit, we cannot understand the mysteries of the Scriptures. The Bible becomes just another book, just another collection of words. The Word is life through the Spirit. There is no understanding of Scripture without the Spirit. There is no revelation without the Spirit.

1 Corinthians 2:6-11 tells us:

*"We do, however, speak a message of wisdom among the mature, but not the wisdom of this age or of the rulers of this age, who are coming to nothing. No, we declare God's wisdom, a mystery that has been hidden and that God destined for our glory before time began. None of the rulers of this age understood it, for if they had, they would not have crucified the Lord of glory. However, as it is written: 'What no eye has seen, what no ear has heard, and what no human mind has conceived' the things God has prepared for those who love him — **these are the things God has revealed to us by his Spirit.** The Spirit searches all things, even the deep things of God. **For who knows a person's thoughts except their own spirit within them?** In the same way no one knows the thoughts of God except the Spirit of God."*

To understand Scripture is to depend solely on the Holy Spirit to impart revelation as we read. Otherwise, we will ***not*** understand what we are reading, or know how to apply it to our lives. It makes no sense reading the Word, without first praying for God's help to understand it.

Take some time to truly meditate on the following

A Glorious Church

Scriptures. Ask Holy Spirit to illuminate your understanding. Read, close your eyes and listen. See if you can identify the voice of God as He tells you how these verses really apply to your life. Write down what you hear, and what you see:

"I can do all things through Christ who strengthens me." - Philippians 4:13

"No, in all these things we are more than conquerors through him who loved us." - Romans 8:37

"For the Word of God is quick, and powerful, and sharper than any two edged sword, piercing even to the dividing asunder of soul and spirit, and of the joints and marrow, and is a discerner of the thoughts and intents of the heart." - Hebrews 4:12

"And without faith it is impossible to please God." - Hebrews 11:6

Each of these verses has a deeper, revelatory meaning that will change your life. That is why it is important for us to make time to study the Word of God, meditate on it, pray and listen to what God has to say.

God reveals himself more to us during personal devotions and time spent with Him, than He does at church. People who pray only when they come to church, read the Bible only when they come to church, witness only when they come to church and give only when they come to church are *religious*. That is exactly what the Scribes and Pharisees used to do.

*God wants a **relationship**, not **religion**.*

If you spend time with God, you will hear His voice. If you begin to obey, your whole life and the very culture of your church will change.

Prophetic Word

The world was built on sound. It exists because of that sound. Sounds release creative vibrations that echo through many generations. If I stop speaking, life will cease to exist. If you stop listening, the silver cord will be loosed. The world moves in a sound. When Adam sinned, I am the One who came looking for him. I am the One who called after him. He heard the sound of me walking towards him. I am the One who spoke to him. I am not silent, but sometimes you don't listen. You surround yourself with the wrong sound. The enemy has tried to duplicate my sound, to imitate my voice, but his words are coated with darkness and instill fear. When I speak, there is peace, joy, hope and love. Listen to me. I can speak through anything I created. All creation echoes my sound. Quiet your spirit and listen. You will hear me speaking.

CHAPTER NINE
Christ in Us

Another alternative title for this Chapter could be, "Abiding in Christ." John 15:1-8 says:

"I am the true vine, and my Father is the husbandman. Every branch in me that beareth not fruit he taketh away: and every branch that beareth fruit, he purgeth it, that it may bring forth more fruit. Now ye are clean through the word which I have spoken unto you. Abide in me, and I in you. As the branch cannot bear fruit of itself, except it abide in the vine; no more can ye, except ye abide in me. I am the vine, ye are the branches: He that abideth in me, and I in him, the same bringeth forth much fruit: for without me ye can do nothing. If a man abide not in me, he is cast forth as a branch, and is withered; and men gather them, and cast them into the fire, and they are burned. If ye abide in me, and my words abide in you, ye shall ask what ye will, and it shall be done unto you. Herein is my Father glorified, that ye bear much fruit; so shall ye be my disciples."

I went to visit a friend once, and we were standing by her gate. She was standing next to an evergreen tree, and she was just plucking the dry branches off and throwing them in the road one by one without even realizing what she was doing it. I found this gesture a very significant one when I read the text in John 15. So, let's talk about trees and branches.

Jesus is the true vine. We are the branches. Keep that in mind as we go through these thoughts. There are some profound lessons to be learnt from the very simple story I just told. In the realm of the spirit, the real world, as members of the body of Christ, we can be attached to the vine and still dry up. We can be attached and still be dead. There can be dead branches on any tree, they are still a part of the tree, but they have no life. If the vine produces life for the branches, how is it possible to have branches that have no life?

There is something in science called Dead-wooding. This is where branches die off for a number of reasons ranging from light deficiency, root damage, to pests and diseases. A dead branch will at some point decay back to the parent stem causing abscission and falling off. Abscission is the natural detachment of parts of a plant, typically dead leaves and ripe fruit or any act of cutting off.

Let us examine these reasons briefly in relation to who we are in Christ:

Light deficiency – We are all exposed to the Son, Jesus Christ. We don't lack light because we are also light (See Matthew 5:14), unless we choose to walk in the darkness.

Root damage – The church has a solid foundation. Jesus said:

"Upon this rock I will build my church and the gates of hell shall not prevail against it." - Matthew 16:18

So, the root of the church is not damaged.

This leaves only one possibility: death by pests and diseases: pests being demons, and diseases being sins. When Christians die, it's either because of the work of satan and his demons or because of sin, or a combination of both.

Dead branches die from the outside in. In order for us to live and be fruitful, we have to draw substance from the vine (in other words, we have to be obedient to God's will), otherwise, we die.

Let us go back to the garden of Eden because when we use words such as *die, dead,* and *dying,* we still think in the physical realm. God said to Adam, *"If you eat of this tree...you will die."* The devil said to the Woman, "You shall not surely die." They ate, but they were still standing, walking, breathing and talking. They did not die physically. The soul that sins will die (See Ezekiel 18:20). Instantly they moved from being a flourishing branch to a dead branch. They were no longer living souls, but dead souls. The same happens to us when we don't abide in Christ.

Very often we commit our sins and find that we are still standing, walking, breathing and talking, so we just continue to sin. But the Word of God says in no uncertain terms that:

C. Orville McLeish

"...the wages of sin is death." - Romans 3:23

When you sin, you transition from being a flourishing branch to being a dead branch on the tree. The serpent continues to convince some of us to eat from the tree of sin because we shall not surely die.

We need to understand that as branches of the life-giving Tree, we have no life of our own. We think we do. We live as if we do. Sometimes we dry up, but because we are still attached to the Tree, we think we are okay. I remember my friends hand reaching out and picking off all the dry branches and casting them aside with little thought or concern.

Anyone who does not abide in Christ is like a branch that is thrown away, gathered up and cast into the fire. That is how we deal with dead branches in the natural.

There is a big difference between being *attached* to Christ and *abiding* in Christ. Every member of the church is attached by association, but only those who abide bear fruit. We are all members of a church, but we are not all bearing fruit, we are not all green and flourishing. Some branches are dead; some are dying.

You can't pretend when you stand in God's presence. When God looks at you, He either sees a fruitful and green branch, a withering branch or a dead branch. God knows who you are, and where you stand.

To abide in Christ means we pray daily. We are always communicating with our Father, seeking His guidance and counsel with all things. God, like any loving Father, wants to be an integral part of our daily lives. To abide in Christ means that we do not leave Him out.

To abide in Christ means that we study God's Word. We are made clean through His Word. We learn His ways and thoughts through His Word. The Word is the only established standard that can reveal what is real, and what is genuine. There is absolutely no substitute for knowing and studying God's Word.

To abide in Christ means that we first seek after God and His righteousness. Everything else takes a back seat. This is easier said than done with a world that demands our attention. Many times, we allow society to set the standard that we live by, but God is calling us to a higher place.

To abide in Christ means that we fast. Fasting teaches us to put flesh under submission. It is the only effective spiritual discipline that I have found to crucify the flesh.

To abide in Christ means that we do not forsake the assembling of ourselves together. In an era of televangelists, we may be tempted to stay at home and participate in an online church program that may appear to be a higher experience than going in person to our local church. While I approve of church in our living rooms, we cannot replace personal fellowship with watching television. I have experienced powerful revelations and had good experiences pointing my hand at the television set, and agreeing with someone praying, but that can never qualify as an assembly.

To abide in Christ means that we take part in the Lord's Supper and feet washing. Allow me to use the Word of God:

> *"For every time you eat this bread and drink this cup, you are announcing the Lord's death until he comes again."* - 1 Corinthians 11:26 – NLT

Once a month would not be considered often enough, bordering on religion instead of spirituality. We can have the Lord's Supper at home with our spouses and family members anytime. I take communion at home every day. As our knowledge increases, we grow in our understanding of what it means to be in a relationship with God, and not just be religious. He never called us to do the same things repeatedly, in the same way, every time.

To abide in Christ means that we love our enemies. We have created a culture of hate, and label it indifference. There are people we merely greet but never hold a conversation with. Jesus eliminated all excuses not to love when He commanded that we love our enemies (See Matthew 5:44).

To abide in Christ means that we run from Potiphar's wife, we offer up praises and pray when we find ourselves in prison, we worship and give thanks when we are persecuted, and we spread the gospel even when our lives are at risk. We must abide in Christ, and Christ will abide in us.

Christ in us means we must bear fruit. In other words, we reproduce our faith in Christ in others; we cannot reproduce what we don't have.

Christ in us means we maintain a right attitude when we go through suffering and difficulties. We are always thankful, under all circumstances (See 1 Thessalonians 5:18). Joseph and Job were wonderful examples. We like how the stories end, but we want to get to the palace without having to go through the pit and prison, but God teaches us through difficulties, and then He blesses us.

Christ in us doesn't mean we somehow control Him, making us free to do as we like. We live in an age where Christians do what they want to do with little or no consideration to what God desires for us.

We don't want to kneel in church anymore. God is still a holy God. He is seeking a remnant of people not afraid to fall on their faces before Him. God is still a consuming fire (See Hebrews 12:29).

Christ in us means we can move mountains, part Red Seas, cast out demons, speak to sickness and people are healed, and defeat giants.

Christ in us means the Holy Spirit is in us. We no longer walk in fear but power, love, and a sound mind (See 2 Timothy 1:7).

Christ in us means if our neighbor needs salvation, Christ can do it through us. It means the hungry can be fed through us, the brokenhearted can be counseled through us, people can be prayed for and touched through us, the gospel can go to all nations through us, and captives can be set free through us. It is a responsibility that Jesus passed to His Church, His Body in the fullness of His Spirit.

Christ in us means we don't have to live in sin. We don't have to abide by worldly culture or be influenced by it. We don't have to fit in at school or at the workplace. We don't need to wear or follow the latest fashion. We don't have to do what everybody else is doing.

Christ in us means we can rise above circumstances and situations that hinder our walk with God. It means we are more than conquerors through Him. It means we can do all things through Him. We don't have to be bound by chains of immorality or depression.

Christ in us means we are citizens of heaven living on earth for a brief time. We don't need to fear death. We don't need to conform to this world. We don't need to fear the fallen principalities and powers.

Christ in us means that everybody around us should be affected and infected with the gospel. It means that people who know us should know Christ.

Christ in us means we have a great responsibility because we carry God almighty in our body.

The Spirit of God is not condemning you; He is calling you.

A Glorious Church

He loves dry branches; they are easy to light with fire. God values honesty and accountability. One of the reasons so many of us struggle and can't find freedom is that we are afraid to say we need help. We are afraid of what people will think and say if they know we struggle with some things.

I was addicted to porn and masturbation for more than half my life, and all my Christian life, until a few years ago. I was so entrenched in the habit that I declared that if God could set me free, He could set anybody free. If you are bound, you can be free. Seek your freedom from Jesus Himself, for who the Son sets free is free indeed (See John 8:36).

Read the Scriptures carefully from the major to the minor prophets and you will see that the church got to a place where the services were being held, songs were being sung, Scriptures were being read, sacrifices were being made as they should, but God was not pleased because the hearts of the people were far from Him. In the book of Amos, he wrote:

"I hate, I despise your religious festivals; your assemblies are a stench to me. Even though you bring me burnt offerings and grain offerings, I will not accept them. Though you bring choice fellowship offerings, I will have no regard for them. Away with the noise of your songs! I will not listen to the music of your harps. But let justice roll on like a river, righteousness like a never-failing stream!"

We see similar passages in the book of Lamentations, but the church was as stubborn then at it is now with too many branches choosing to live according to the flesh instead of the Spirit. There are many Christians who are in love with this world. Our love for the world; the music, the lifestyle, the culture, is destroying the witness of the church.

God is calling His Church to righteousness. God is calling His Church back to holiness. We need to rid our lives of the inconsistencies. God desires complete surrender; otherwise, we are just playing church.

"...If you remain in me and I in you, you will bear much fruit; apart from me you can do nothing." - St. John 15:5

Prayer

Dear God,
There are so many things I can do, or not do. I can sit and do nothing, or I can attempt to do many things. Please show me, Lord, what you would have me to do. I am open to your leading and willing for You to work through me to accomplish Your will. Whether my purpose is to accomplish something small or great, I know that it is important to the work of Your Kingdom and Your plan for my life. Please guide and direct me, and bring me into the fullness of what it means to have Christ in me. In the name of Jesus, I pray, Amen.

Jesus Prays For You

Father, the hour has come. glorify your Son that your Son

may glorify you. For You granted him authority over all people that he might give eternal life to all those You have given him. Now this is eternal life: that they know You, the only true God, and Jesus Christ, whom You have sent. I have brought You glory on earth by finishing the work You gave me to do. And now, Father, glorify me in Your presence with the glory I had with You before the world began. I have revealed You to those whom You gave me out of the world. They were Yours; You gave them to me, and they have obeyed Your Word. Now they know that everything You have given me comes from You. For I gave them the words You gave me, and they accepted them. They knew with certainty that I came from You, and they believed that You sent me. I pray for them. I am not praying for the world, but for those You have given me, for they are Yours. All I have is Yours, and all You have is mine. And glory has come to me through them. I will remain in the world no longer, but they are still in the world, and I am coming to You. Holy Father protect them by the power of Your name, the name You gave me so that they may be one as we are one. While I was with them, I protected them and kept them safe by that name You gave me. None has been lost except the one doomed to destruction so that Scripture would be fulfilled. I am coming to You now, but I say these things while I am still in the world so that they may have the full measure of my joy within them. I have given them Your Word and the world has hated them, for they are not of the world any more than I am of the world. My prayer is not that You take them out of the world but that You protect them from the evil one. They are not of the world, even as I am not of it. Sanctify them by the truth; Your Word is truth. As You sent me into the world, I have sent them into the world. For them, I sanctify myself, that they too may be truly sanctified. My prayer is not for them alone. I pray also for those who will believe in me through their message, that all of them may be one, Father, just as You are in me and I am in You. May they also be in us so that the world may believe that You have sent me. I have given them the glory that You gave me, that they may be one as we are one— I in them and You in me—so that they may be brought to complete unity. Then the world will know that You sent me and have loved them even as You have loved me. Father, I want those You have given me to be with me where I am, and to see my glory, the glory You have given me because You loved me before the creation of the world. Righteous Father, though the world does not know You, I know You, and they know that You have sent me. I have made You known to them, and will continue to make You known in order that the love You have for me may be in them and that I myself may be in them (John 17:1-26).

CHAPTER TEN
The Power of a Transformed Mind

Recently, I heard a question asked during a local youth ministry meeting, "How do we represent Jesus?" Several answers were given, but I was listening for a specific list but never heard it.

The answer to the question for me is that we are to do the same things Jesus did. What did Jesus do? He healed the sick, raised the dead, cast out demons and proclaimed liberty to those who were bound. He told us to go and do likewise.

For the fun of it, I have ministered in several churches and mentioned that we have the power and authority to raise people from the dead. The look on people's faces suggested that they really didn't know what to do with a thought like that. Most of us have never seen blind eyes opened, deaf ears opened or heard the mute speak. We have never seen demons casts out of a mad person on the streets, or witnessed their sanity return with the absence of the evil spirits. And I talk about raising the dead! If we have a hard time processing what Jesus says we can do, then the problem must be within our minds.

Romans 12:2 is significant if we are to move into the realm and reality of a glorious Church. It will never manifest until we can first see it in our minds and believe that it is possible. The church may never advance until we address this pressing issue.

How Kingdom-conscious are we?

We serve a supernatural God. That is His nature. Why are we not seeing a manifestation of the nature of God? This is the question I have been petitioning my God with for months. If, Thou Art Christ, the Son of the Living God, then why is today's church so different from the church I read about in Acts, the church that was founded on the rock?

God has led me to book after book, experience after experience, people after people, revelation after revelation in my relentless pursuit of His manifested glory and it all boils down to one thing: my mindset.

"Do not conform to the pattern of this world, but be transformed by the renewing of your mind. Then you will be able to test and approve what God's will is—his good, pleasing and perfect will." - Romans 12:2

Who was Paul writing to? Romans 1:7 tells us:

"To all in Rome who are loved by God and called to be his holy people:"

Why did Paul need to tell Christians who were forgiven, saved, sanctified and filled with the Holy Ghost that they needed to renew their minds?

A Glorious Church

We know there is a need for salvation. We are all born in sin because of the sin of Adam. When Adam sinned, man became a dead soul. Our soul is connected to God by the Spirit, so that connection was severed. The second Adam restored what was lost. He came to save our souls. In accepting Christ, we are made new, which suggest that we receive a new soul. We once again became a living soul, but our body remains the same. We retained the memory of sin in our body. We retained our old mindset. When I was baptized in water at seventeen (I think), I walked home with my hand on a girl's breast. Being immersed in water did not change my mindset. That is why Galatians 5:16 tells us who are saved:

"Walk according to the spirit and not the flesh."

It is possible to walk in the flesh as a Christian. A lot of Christians do because when we get saved, there is still some work to be done.

Jesus did a massive work over 2,000 years ago and established a church on the principles of power and authority that we have failed to carry down throughout the centuries. The Holy Spirit came to give life to those who belong to Christ. In essence, He made us one with our Lord.

My prayer is not for them alone. I pray also for those who will believe in me through their message, that all of them may be one, Father, just as you are in me and I am in you. May they also be in us so that the world may believe that you have sent me. I have given them the glory that you gave me, that they may be one as we are one— I in them and you in me—so that they may be brought to complete unity. Then the world will know that you sent me and have loved them even as you have loved me. - John 17: 20-23

We are one with God through the Holy Spirit. We are one Spirit with Jesus. The Holy Spirit also brings to our life God's individual plans and purposes. These were established before the foundations of the world. God says:

"Before I formed you in the womb I knew you, before you were born I set you apart; I appointed you as a prophet to the nations." - Jeremiah 1:5

David got a glimpse of God's thoughts towards each of us and boldly declared:

"How precious to me are your thoughts, God! How vast is their sum! If I would count them, they are more in number than the sand. When I wake up, I am still with you." - Psalm 139:17-18

The Holy Spirit brings into our lives the mind of Christ, suggesting that there are at least two minds co-existing within each of us.

Our natural minds naturally hate the things of God. It really doesn't want to have anything to do with God because it is ruled by our ego (false self), and if we allow this mind to have dominion over us, the Kingdom of God cannot flow through us. The result is that we pray for the sick in Jesus name, and nothing happens. We tell demons to leave in Jesus name, and nothing happens. Our minds must be brought under submission to a greater mindset for the glory of God to flow through us:

"...be transformed by the renewing of your mind." - Romans 12:2

The original word used for "renewing" also means to "renovate." When you renovate, what do you do? You refurbish, repair, mend, fix up, remodel. How is this accomplished?

"Let this mind be in you, which was also in Christ Jesus." - Philippians 2:5

The use of the word *let* suggest that we are to allow. The mind of Christ is already present, so we just need to give permission by an act of our will.

Jesus once spoke to a fig tree, and it dried up. He used that as a lesson of faith. If we speak it and have no doubt, it will manifest.

As a church, we talk a lot, but there is no manifestation because we are thinking from a mind that is convinced that the dead cannot be raised, demons are to be feared and sickness is a part of living. Our minds block the flow of God's Kingdom that is right here in our midst. It is not so much that we think negatively, but we think with the wrong mind.

The devil is fine with us walking after our own thoughts. He trembles when we start to walk after the thoughts of the Spirit. We are to:

*"Cast down imaginations, and every high thing that exalteth itself against the knowledge of God, and bringing into captivity **every** thought to the obedience of Christ."* - 2 Corinthians 10:5 (emphasis mine)

To be more practical, and I use myself as an example, my carnal mind has no tolerance for gospel music, preaching, the Word of God, witnessing, testifying, holiness or righteousness. My mind has a problem if the Scripture being read is too long, and the message is too long.

Seldom are we willing to admit the real truth, as it relates to our inner man because very often we sell a distorted image of who we really are to our peers and those we interact with.

My mind believes that God can only provide money that I work for, cancer kills, AIDS kills, demons cannot be cast out or they don't exist, sickness is a part of God's plan for our lives, and the blind, deaf and lame will always be blind, deaf and lame. The reality is that I have accepted that a man who has been amputated will remain in that state all his natural life. This is the reality that we have been taught growing up. We know that there were three Hebrew boys who were once cast into a fire and came out unsinged without even the smell of smoke. The thought of a God who delivers from fires and lions is good, but we don't ever want to walk through fire or be cast before lions.

A Glorious Church

I have always said that everyone loves the end product, but not the process.

It is the process that we have missed as a church, where the theory we believe is literally tested to see if it is true or false. It is during the process that we pray, *"Thy will be done on earth, as it is in heaven."* There is no sickness, cancer, AIDS, or one-foot man in heaven. There is no poverty or death. We pray, *"Thy Kingdom come."* We pray, *"For thine is the kingdom, the power and the glory."* We say, *"The enemy is under our feet,"* yet we are afraid, and we don't believe. We say, "Greater is He who is in me than he that is in the world," and we still conform to the ideas and practices of this world because we are fearful we will lose our jobs or lives. What we say conflicts with how we think because our minds are not yet transformed.

A transformed mind knows that:

"Nothing is impossible for God" (See Luke 1:37).

"We have the keys to the kingdom" (See Matthew 16:19).

"We are carriers of the power and Glory of God in this world, because the Holy Spirit who moved upon the waters in Genesis lives in us" (See Romans 8:11).

"Even if we walk through the valley of the shadow of death, we will fear no evil" (See Psalm 23:4).

C. Orville McLeish

"The Kingdom of God is within us" (See Luke 17:21).

"We can do the same things Christ did and even greater things" (See John 14:12).

"We are far above all principality, and power, and might, and dominion, and every name that is named, not only in this world, but also in that which is to come" (See Ephesians 1:21).

"Sickness and disease are subjected to us" (See St. Matthew 8:17).

"We will not fear the terror by night, nor the arrow that flieth by day" (See Psalm 91:5).

"We can raise the dead" (See Matthew 10:8).

"We can single handed rout 1,000 demons or men" (See Joshua 23:10).

"We have the Spirit of power, love and sound mind" (See 2 Timothy 1:7).

"We are above only and never beneath" (See Deuteronomy 28:13).

"We are the head and not the tail" (See Deuteronomy 28:13).

"Everywhere our feet touches belong to us" (See Joshua 1:3).

"Anything we put our hands to will prosper" (See Deuteronomy 30:9).

"The wealth of the wicked is stored up for us" (See Proverbs 13:22).

Any thought that opposes these promises or seeks to cast doubt is not from God. These are some of His promises to us, uttered from His mouth, and if we dare to believe them, we will eventually see them manifest.

"The Lord said to me, "You have seen correctly, for I am watching to see that my Word is fulfilled." - Jeremiah 1:12

Whatever God says, He will do. He watches over His Word to perform it. Despite the realities of our circumstances and situations right now, just believe God.

If we want to experience the nature of our supernatural God, we need to have a different mindset. We need to have the same mind as Christ and think our thoughts after Him.

When God said that His ways are not our ways, nor His thoughts our thoughts (See Isaiah 55:8-9), He was not saying that we can never think like Him. He was saying we will never experience God through our own thoughts, but He has put His thoughts in us (which is much higher) so we can think like Him, experience Him, speak like Him and truly represent Him in this earth. We need to become like Jesus to everyone we meet daily. That is what it truly means to bring heaven to earth.

C. Orville McLeish

Prophetic Word

Beloved, if you think from the perspective of this world, you will never understand My world or My Word. They speak of a higher realm the natural mind cannot comprehend. I am a Spirit, and I honor and perform My Word in the Spirit. I have healed you, restored you, redeemed you, and prospered you in your heavenly position, but you have the responsibility to bring the realities of My world into your world. I have commissioned, equipped and commanded you to do it. The natural world is not the dominant reality, for it will give way to that which is eternal. Rise up, sons. Rise up, daughters. Sit with me in heavenly places. Your seat is already prepared. You don't have to be oppressed and tormented when I have prepared a table before you with the peace that surpasses understanding, and joy that will give strength to your bones. You don't have to allow sickness to ravish your bodies or live out your lives in lack. The price has been paid. You must learn to appropriate it in your own lives. I am calling you to a higher place, a higher reality, one that is more real and powerful than that which you know. Arise, body of Christ. Arise, burning ones. Arise, glorious light!

CHAPTER ELEVEN
Maximize Your Potential

Before you can speak on certain topics, you must live them. I never dreamed in all my years as a Christian that I could stand at a pulpit and speak a word. If you knew anything about me, the thought would have been hilarious, to put it mildly. One day, I was driving alone in my car as a young man and had a vision of me standing at a pulpit and preaching up a storm. People were falling on their faces before God and experiencing a full manifestation of God's glory. I did what any normal Christian youth would do when God shows them a glimpse of what they would become. I laughed.

As I grew older and wiser, I considered what would matter when I looked back over my life as I neared the end of my earthly life. What legacy would I leave behind for the generations that come after? We all want to hear *"...Well done thou good and faithful servant"* (See Matthew 25:23) but what would I do to deserve getting to hear those words?

I think about a lot of things, and as a writer, I often lose touch with reality because there are too many stories swimming around in my head, too much to write. There are unsaved people living in sin, and someone needs to reach them. There are Christians who have no idea what the Word teaches, and someone needs to reach them.

Eventually, I became the image I saw in my mind, and now resolve that "God can do anything" and "God can use anyone."

"I can do everything through him who gives me strength." - Philippians 4:13

I looked up the meaning of *everything*, and it was defined as *anything*. I looked up the meaning of *anything* and saw this definition: *used to refer to a thing, no matter what.* In essence, it doesn't matter what that thing is, you can do it through Christ.

We often limit God and make bold statements in how we live and the choices we make, and we send a message to others that God cannot perform on His promises. When the bills need to be paid, we get a loan. When the doctor says we are sick, and there is no cure, we give up, roll over and die.

"...with God all things are possible." - Matthew 19:26

I have lived most of my Christian life quoting that Scripture, getting excited when I heard it preached, but not believing it. Surely all things are possible, except...

We have created doctrines based on our limited experiences, and even interpreted Scriptures on our experiences. Doing so has somehow diminished who God is, and who we are in Him.

The quality of our lives will always be determined by what we believe. God's question to me over the last few years has been very simple, "Do you dare to believe God?"

God's reality, where He thinks and speaks, is a higher reality than the one we are presently living. Many people may be content with that, but some are not. Those who refuse to conform to anything less than what God has spoken will have a greater impact on the world. They will learn to maximize their potential and live their lives as sons of God instead of mere natural human beings. Not to say we are to ignore our natural existence, but if the natural came out of the supernatural (unseen world), then we should prioritize our spiritual existence, and live from that perspective. If we can accomplish that, a lot of things will change.

Potential means *capable of being or becoming.* Each of us has a potential to be. I was quiet by nature and loved to work behind the scenes. I disliked being up in the front, but God knew I had the potential to teach Bible Study. I did not know, but God did. I did not know I could be a published author, best-selling playwright, self-publishing expert, produced screenwriter in the United States and Australia, and have all manner of clients from every stratosphere of life. If I told you what God has done in and through my life all over this world, you would not believe me. I am nothing. Just a small-town country boy who dared to believe God, and obeyed His leading over the years, without even realizing I was doing it. God knew I had the potential to deliver a message on Sunday, write award-winning plays and change lives. I didn't. I saw myself doing it in my head, but surely I could not do it in reality. Am I any different from anybody reading this? No! Did I do something that you can't do? No! There is a process that needs to take place before you can realize your full potential, but I just want to establish first that when God formed you in the womb, He put greatness inside you, and we all have the ability to do great things.

Jeremiah 1:1-10 says:

The words of Jeremiah son of Hilkiah, one of the priests at Anathoth in the territory of Benjamin. The word of the Lord came to him in the thirteenth year of the reign of Josiah son of Amon king of Judah, and through the reign of Jehoiakim son of Josiah king of Judah, down to the fifth month of the eleventh year of Zedekiah son of Josiah king of Judah, when the people of Jerusalem went into exile. The word of the Lord came to me, saying, "Before I formed you in the womb I knew you, before you were born I set you apart; I appointed you as a prophet to the nations." "Ah, Sovereign Lord," I said, "I do not know how to speak; I am only a child." But the Lord said to me, "Do not say, 'I am only a child.' You must go to everyone I send you to and say whatever I command you. Do not be afraid of them, for I am with you and will rescue you," declares the Lord. Then the Lord reached out his hand and touched my mouth and said to me, "Now, I have put my words in your mouth. See, today I appoint you over nations and kingdoms to uproot and tear down, to destroy and overthrow, to build and to plant." (NIV).

We were called to do much more than just exist or survive. What we have inside us is the potential to be and do anything.

A Glorious Church

God is our source and qualification, and He lives inside us. That is potential, and we all have it.

Hebrews 12:2 says:

"Looking unto Jesus the author and finisher of our faith; who for the joy that was set before him endured the cross, despising the shame, and is set down at the right hand of the throne of God." (KJV).

One of the greatest limitations that we have is not hearing the voice of the Lord, who speaks to us every day.

The story is told of a woman who God told to full a kitchen sink with water and sit in it. She obeyed. Three gunmen broke into the house, and only God knew their intent. When they saw her sitting in the water in the kitchen sink, they thought she was mad, so they left. We need to know God's voice as He possesses the keys to unlock our full potential.

From the moment we got saved, we have been on a path loaded with potential. But we ignore it, or we are afraid to face it.

"For God hath not given us the spirit of fear; but of power, and of love, and of a sound mind." - 2 Timothy 1:7 – KJV

Let us be realistic and honest: Have you ever imagined yourself doing something that you see as impossible? Have you ever seen yourself delivering a powerful word, giving a powerful testimony, praying a prayer so strong demons flee, atmosphere changes, people are healed? Have you ever seen yourself ministering to non-Christians with such effectiveness that they practically run to Jesus? Have you ever seen yourself influencing communities, nations, the world? I want to tell you today that if you have seen it or thought about it, you have the potential to do it. You have a choice to maximize on your gifts or to bury them, thereby producing nothing. You have the gift, but you can choose never to develop or use it (See Matthew 25:13-30).

Your gifts were given to you so you can impact the world of which you are a part for God. If you refuse to use them, you will not only answer to God for burying them but for everybody else whose salvation depended on your living up to your fullest potential in God. Yes, we are our brother's keeper. There is no getting away from that responsibility. We are God's eyes, ears, hands, and feet. We still have Jonahs among us who are running or hiding.

Jesus tells a story in Matthew 25 of a man preparing to leave on a long journey who entrusts his possessions to his servants. He distributes his wealth among three servants, apportioned to them on the basis of their abilities. To the first he entrusted five talents, to the second two talents, and to the third one talent. The first two servants quickly set to work with their master's money. The third servant did not invest his master's money at all; he dug a hole in the ground and buried it. When the master returned, the first two eagerly met their master, apparently delighted in the opportunity to multiply their master's money. Both were commended as good and faithful servants; both were rewarded with increased responsibilities in their master's service; both were invited to share in their master's joy.

The master's dealing with the third servant was a different matter. This servant came to his master with only the talent his master had originally entrusted to him. He did not increase his master's money at all. In fact, if this were to take place today, that money would likely have lost value due to inflation. The servant offered a feeble excuse for his conduct. He told his master that he was a harsh and cruel man, a man who was demanding, and who expected gain where he had not labored. He contended that this was why he was afraid to take a risk with any kind of investment, so he simply hid the money, and now he returned it without any gain. The master rebuked this slave for being evil and lazy. He took his talent from him and gave it to the one who earned ten. Matthew 25:29-30 goes on to say that:

"For to everyone who has will more be given, and he will have an abundance. But from the one who has not, even what he has will be taken away. And cast the worthless servant into the outer darkness. In that place there will be weeping and gnashing of teeth."

We should carefully note the outcome of faithful service, and of unfaithful service, in this parable. Faithful service leads to increased responsibilities in the Kingdom of heaven and eternal joy in the presence of the Master, Jesus Christ. Unfaithful service leads to condemnation, the removal of one's stewardship, and an eternity of weeping and gnashing of teeth in outer darkness, away from the presence of our Lord.

We run because we don't want the increased responsibility. Increased responsibility means accountability, and accountability means we can't live our lives our own way. We have a responsibility to carry this gospel to everyone who needs it.

Mark 16:15 says:

"And he said unto them, go ye into all the world, and preach the Gospel to every creature."

God is not seeking great men, but normal people who will do great things. What are you leaving for the generation to come? What will you be remembered for? What legacy will you leave for your children?

I was raised in an average Jamaican home. We didn't have more than enough. We had enough: shelter over our heads (nothing elaborate), food on the table, clothes on our backs, and shoes on our feet. When I got saved, I wore the same pants and shoes to church every Sunday. My parents could not afford to take any of their children beyond grade 11. We all knew that was where the buck would stop. My mother had nine children (three sets of three – I am in the last set with my father), and my father had five (two with his first wife). My father died of prostate cancer in 2012 (the year I got married). He was eighty, and all he left behind was a house in need of renovating, and a good size property. We have all struggled through life with the legacy of *never enough*, and *barely enough* until I boldly declared *enough was enough*. I made a conscious decision that I would not continue the legacy my father left. He was on medication for more than half his life, and never experienced a higher quality of life. Even his mental health deteriorated with time, and I am sure his departure was a relief for some, though death is never something we are prepared for. I know I have initiated a war to battle the same mindset that held him in that place all his life because I want my children to inherit something better.

Living at your maximum potential is never just for you; it is for others, and especially those who will come after you. I am going to do something my parents never did, and that is to pay for my children to go to college. I will probably also buy their first car, if I feel like it. Some may say they will not learn to be responsible, but from experience, it is enough to maintain a car, purchase gas, and pay bills. If they had to work in our present economy to buy a house and a car, they would be locked in a job all their lives that they might not enjoy, and never achieve their maximum potential. That is what we inherited. Do you really want to pass that on to your children? My heart goes out to those who are stuck in a nine-to-five job because they very rarely get to operate at their greatest potential. My encouragement is that you find a way to turn your passion into a profitable business. I believe this is God's heart for us.

We all received a mandate when we got saved. We have been redeemed, restored and adopted into the family of God, a position we were all predestined to occupy. It was never intended to be something you keep to yourselves. Have you ever been in love and tried to keep it a secret? How do you keep the secret to eternal life and true freedom to yourselves when you know your neighbor, your brother, or your sister will forever be separated from God, if they deny Him? You are responsible for them, and you will have to give an account.

We have potential prophets, discerners, prayer warriors, preachers, singers, evangelists, and apostles in us and among us. God wants to bring these gifts out but in order for there to be more of God, there has to be less of us.

Some people are good with graphics, and some can write poems and stories, but they use the gifts only to get through high school and colleges, then they bury them. I am talking about having the potential to be great and doing nothing. We say, "I can't" or "I don't want to" when God tell us that we can, and we should. There is really no such thing as "I can't." Either you don't want to, or you don't know how to. You can easily identify someone who has abandoned the path to a greater existence. They say things like, "I used to." God gave much. He is always serving, always giving, always loving, and at no point will He ever say, "I used to."

"Jesus Christ is the same yesterday and today and forever." - Hebrews 13:8

It is time for us as a church, and as members of the body of Christ, to give something back.

A Glorious Church

There are five things that stop us from achieving our maximum potential.

- Fear
- Sin
- Doubt
- Inconsistency
- Lack of Endurance

I have addressed most of these issues in the previous chapters.

There are three things I consistently pray for, hope for and expect:

- Divine health
- Divine wealth
- That my faith produces the same results here on earth as Jesus' faith produced

In John 14:12, Jesus says that we will do greater works than He did. We are living in the *greater works* era. If we don't take dominion and subdue this earth as its rightful heirs, then it will be ruled by the dominion of darkness. We will always be sick, broke, lacking all good things, never achieving, always suppressed, oppressed and tormented. Jesus calls us to a higher place, and He has done all He can do to reposition and realign us with our true calling and purpose in Him, but we must believe that it is already done and live from that place of rest and victory. It is the enemy's intention to recreate the world as it existed before Jesus came in the flesh, and have us live from that place of hopelessness, fear, and defeat. It is not the reality of the heavenly places, but a state of mind.

"Praise be to the God and Father of our Lord Jesus Christ, who has blessed us in the heavenly realms with every spiritual blessing in Christ." - Ephesians 1:3 – NIV

If we don't believe it, we will never access it.

"...in all these things we are more than conquerors through him who loved us." Romans 8:37 – NIV

If we don't believe it, we will never be it.

Read the Scriptures to believe; believe to become; become to overcome and overcome to reign with Jesus Christ.

Prophetic Word

My ways are not your ways, neither are My thoughts your thoughts. I see this world through a different lens. Your peripheral vision has been compromised. You must look through My eyes if you desire to know the truth about Me, and about yourself. You are more than you think, more than you believe about yourself. You have the potential to do great and mighty acts, just as all the men and women you read about in My Word. Just as My Son Jesus did. You are My son. Jesus has made the way for you to walk in. Walk therefore in the way. Do not turn to the left, or to the right. Do not turn back. Press forward in the truth. You know the truth. The truth lives inside you. Pay attention to the truth and follow the voice of Truth. Do not settle for a lie. Do not give ear to the father of lies. Lies enslave your mind and keep you bound in a state of powerlessness, sickness and weakness. I called you to be bold, strong, healthy and prosperous. Every Word that I have spoken in the Bible is for you. That is the only way.

CHAPTER TWELVE
Back to the Garden of Eden

The spiritual realm is far more complex than our natural minds can comprehend. It speaks of a glory that was, is and is to come. The victory that exists for all sons of God is that what was, will be once again. We are going back to the garden of Eden.

I received this revelation on Sunday, February 5, 2011, long before I even knew I would be a published author. So, let me begin by saying that outside the written and established Word of God, there is no truth. It is the only standard by which we can judge truth. I realized then that to know what was coming, I needed to look at what was.

Salvation is a story that begins in Genesis, and we often think it ends in Revelation, but it doesn't. We need to treat the Bible like a novel. We don't open a novel, go to the middle, read a sentence and know what that novel is about. Simply put, the Bible is about Creation, Fall, and Creation Anew. In essence, the revealing of the sons of God begins in Genesis and ends in Genesis.

God created man in His own image. Let us carefully examine

what it was like then. How would you define the existence of a man then?

"Then God said, 'Let us make mankind in our image, in our likeness, so that they may rule over the fish in the sea and the birds in the sky, over the livestock and all the wild animals, and over all the creatures that move along the ground.' So God created mankind in his own image, in the image of God he created them; male and female he created them. God blessed them and said to them, 'Be fruitful and increase in number, fill the earth and subdue it. Rule over the fish in the sea and the birds in the sky and over every living creature that moves on the ground.'" - Genesis 1:26-28

In addition to our responsibilities, we see other aspects of life before sin:

"Then the man and his wife heard the sound of the Lord God as he was walking in the garden in the cool of the day..." - Genesis 3:8 – NIV

Before sin, we got a glimpse of God's original intention. We see what a relationship with God looked like. He came down to us. It was never about us going to God. The idea that we are on our way to heaven is an escape mentality that causes us to miss the whole point. We are not going to God. God is coming to us. We came from God, but we got lost. God has come looking for humanity. "Adam, where are you?"

Sin damaged the original plan, created a detour, and distorted the image of God in humanity. Now there needed to be a new plan. Creation had been compromised; the Creator now has to re-create. We need to understand that while humanity continues to live out their existence, most in ignorance and lacking in knowledge of the truth and identity, God has been working out His ultimate plan in the hearts and lives of many people. We have desires without knowing their origins. Very often we are set on an irreversible path towards God without being aware of our journey until we find ourselves at a place that literally surprises us. I say that because it happened to me. How I started writing books was a journey I never embarked on. Humanity's journey will end with the establishment of a new heaven and a new earth, in essence, back in the garden of Eden.

We often say that God came to earth to restore all things. This statement is confirmed by the Word in Acts 3:21:

"Heaven must receive him until the time comes for God to restore everything, as he promised long ago through his holy prophets."

You cannot restore something that never was. The work of the Holy Spirit within us is one of prominence. He is changing us from the inside out back into the perfect image of God. This is already a complete work in our new soul, but not yet in our body.

On this journey back to the garden of Eden (new heaven, new earth), we think about resurrection and somehow think it is different from the resurrection of Christ. We think we will receive a new body that is somehow different from this old body. The body will be different but the same body. The earth will be different but the same earth.

The Bible is filled with types and shadows. In its pages, we clearly see the journey we are taking. We see God giving everything to help us get back to our original design; His original intention. We see God encountering man, fellowshipping with man, dying for man, and we also see our own stubbornness toward the work of God in us. Technology might have increased. Knowledge might have increased. But it's the same journey.

The Israelites wandered around in the desert because they loved Egypt more than what God had in store for them. They had never been to this promised land; they didn't know what to expect, what it would be like, how it would smell, what kind of food would be there. Sounds familiar? They knew Egypt, and they were content enough to want to go back there. Their minds were stuck in Egypt. They wanted to go back. In the same way, we want things to remain as they are because we struggle to comprehend a new and different world. We have no memory of what it was before we came here, so we don't know what to expect. We don't know what it will be like. Our minds are stuck in this world, and man has been wandering in the desert for over 2,000 years because of it. We don't want to leave. Christians dread the future and the new earth when we should be the happiest people in the world. The day we die or get translated should be the best day of our lives. We get to see Jesus for who He really is without limits.

Paul says it best in Romans 8:18:

"I consider that our present sufferings are not worth comparing with the glory that will be revealed in us."

"For our present troubles are small and won't last very long. Yet they produce for us a glory that vastly outweighs them and will last forever!" - 2 Corinthians 4:17 – NLT

Beloved, the future is something to look forward to with eager expectation, not something to dread. If you truly knew what was inside you, your present will change dramatically, and your past would be rendered irrelevant. If Paul is right, and I believe he is, there is nothing that we can experience in this life that will ever compare to the glory that will be revealed in you and me.

Jesus has made it possible for us to begin to experience the garden of Eden today, as Moses did under the old Covenant, as Jesus did on the Mount of Transfiguration. There is a reality greater than the seen world with infinitely more possibilities than we could ask for, think about or imagine. For those who have seen a glimpse into the spiritual world, they have reported that the colors were more vivid, and what they saw and heard was beyond words or explanation. They struggled to describe what they saw.

C. Orville McLeish

I was caught up to the third heaven fourteen years ago. Whether I was in my body or out of my body, I don't know— only God knows. Yes, only God knows whether I was in my body or outside my body. But I do know that I was caught up to paradise and heard things so astounding that they cannot be expressed in words, things no human is allowed to tell. - 2 Corinthians 12:2-4 – NLT

This is a reality and an experience reserved for you, as a son and daughter of God. We are wrong to measure reality by our limited experiences. We are wrong to root our faith in what we can see. A lot of our perceptions have been warped by deception. The enemy has subtly caused us to believe the opposite of what is true in many areas. Theology teaches us that we must interpret the Bible based on who it was written to at the time it was written. The Spirit of God says to interpret the Bible as if it was written for and to you. We are all on the same journey, being led by the same Spirit, with ultimately the same destination in mind. There is no need to make it more complicated than it is.

I want to close this chapter with a closer examination of the attitudes of the Disciples and Apostles. If not stated, you would never know that they were beaten almost to death on numerous occasions, shipwrecked, locked away in prisons and dungeons, stoned, persecuted terribly on levels unimaginable. Yet, it is their words that give us so much hope today, their words that we live by. How did they function under such circumstances, and maintain hope and faith? We struggle when there is not enough money, and when we go through bouts of sickness. We need to assume a better perspective of who we are as children of God.

"But you are a chosen people, a royal priesthood, a holy nation, God's special possession, that you may declare the praises of him who called you out of darkness into his wonderful light." - 1 Peter 2:9

Prophetic Word

I am restoring all things, says the Lord. I have reserved this journey specifically for you. The enemy was not winning. On the contrary, I am working out My perfect plan in your life. The fact that I can get this word to you is a testimony that I can make a way for you, I can make provision you, I see you, and know how to take care of you. You are always on My mind. I have never forgotten you, never left you, never abandoned you, never shunned you, never walked away from you. You are My child. I want to meet you in My garden. We don't need to talk, just you being there is enough for Me. I am your Father. Let me be a Father to you. Sit with Me by the river, eat from the tree of life and be healed. Share your heart with Me. I miss the fellowship we shared before you were born into the earth. Come to Me, and let Me give you rest.

CHAPTER THIRTEEN
A Glorious Church

I am a student of the Word. My life changed when I started reading the Word every day. I often tell people that you don't even need to understand what you are reading for the Word to take effect in your life. Just read! It's a very simple habit that produces great results, and the enemy knows it. He will do what it takes to convince you not to read, and when you don't read, you will believe all kinds of foolishness, and this is one of the things we struggle with as leaders.

One of my favourite books of the Bible is Acts of the Apostles. I turn to the book of Acts, and I read about the early church. When I get to Chapter 28, it is obvious that Acts is the only incomplete book in the Bible. Have you ever watched a movie that ends prematurely, leaving you thinking, "Where's the rest?" The Spirit of the Lord spoke to me, "The church should have continued writing the book of Acts."

I turn to the book of Revelation. I see the Lord writing to the seven churches in the last days. The Lord identified where the church was going right, but then on each occasion, He said, "Yet I hold this against you…" or "Nevertheless, I have a few things against you…" or "Nevertheless, I have this against you…" or "Wake up!" or "I know your deeds…"

"To the one who is victorious, I will give the right to sit with me on my throne, just as I was victorious and sat down with my Father on his throne." - Revelation 3:21

"Here I am!" Says the Lord, "I stand at the door and knock. If anyone hears my voice and opens the door, I will come in and eat with that person and they with me." - Revelation 3:20

So I say, "Lord, what are you saying to us as a church?" And He says, "I stand at the door and knock…"

"What do you mean?"

"That is where I am with a lot of today's churches. I am standing outside the door knocking, but they don't let Me in."

The 21st century church has learnt to have church without God. We know how to look like we are worshipping, and look like we are praying, and look like we are living righteously when our hearts are far from God. How do I know that we are not where we are supposed to be? I know because there are no signs following those who believe, which suggest there is a 'believing' problem. God has not changed.

One day I was so depressed, I said "Lord, I don't like going to church. I am so tired of the tradition and rituals."

And the Lord said, "I don't like to go either."

I turn to Ephesians 5:25-27:

A Glorious Church

"Husbands, love your wives, even as Christ also loved the church, and gave himself for it; That he might sanctify and cleanse it with the washing of water by the word, That he might present it to himself a Glorious Church, not having spot, or wrinkle, or any such thing; but that it should be holy and without blemish."

A *Glorious Church*. I responded, "Lord I want to be a part of this glorious Church." The glorious Church has power and authority over sickness, death and poverty. They lacked nothing!

It was Peter who said: "Silver and gold I do not have. But such as I have, such as I possess, such as was given to me, I freely give to you. In the name of Jesus, get up and walk." (See Acts 3:6 – emphasis mine).

A *Glorious Church* was resounding in my spirit. On top of that, I kept hearing messages being preached in our churches about the glorious Church and walking in the Spirit. I realized that we did have the theology but lacked the experience.

I thought about leaving my church to find this glorious Church, and the Lord said, "Church of God of Prophecy can be that church. You will play a part in the paradigm shift that is coming for this church." Every opportunity I get to teach or preach, I realize the message I deliver very rarely speaks to where the church is, but speaks to where the church should be: A *Glorious Church*.

C. Orville McLeish

"I appoint unto you a kingdom..." - Luke 22:29

"...the knowledge of the secrets of the Kingdom of heaven has been given to you..." - Matthew 13:11

"I will give you the keys of the kingdom of heaven; whatever you bind on earth will be bound in heaven, and whatever you loose on earth will be loosed in heaven." - Matthew 16:19

"The secret of the Kingdom of God has been given to you..." - Mark 4:11

"Thy Kingdom come...Thy will be done on Earth as it is in heaven." - Matthew 6:10

Even though a community can make a big difference, I want this book to speak to you as an individual, because one person can also make a big difference. Every time God acted in a mighty way on the earth, He found a man to work through. God has been looking for you for some time now. He needs you for what He wants to accomplish on earth through you. His mighty hands have been on your life.

God appointed a man on earth to act on His behalf to deliver the children of Israel from Egypt. Moses began to question God, "What if they do not believe me or listen to me and say, 'The Lord did not appear to you?'" God answered his question, with a question, "What do you have in your hand?" Moses carried a staff in his hand because he tended to sheep.

A Glorious Church

What stands out in my mind most about Moses' staff was that when they were standing on the shores of the Red Sea and Pharaoh's army was closing in on them, and the people started to protest, God said to Moses, in Exodus 14:15-16, "Why come to me, go...Lift thou up thy rod, and stretch out thine hand over the sea, and divide it." The message is simple. I have already given you what you need to demonstrate My power here on earth; I have given you the kingdom...

What is the kingdom? 1 Corinthians 4:20:

"For the Kingdom of God is not a matter of talk, but of power."

When Jesus came to earth, He brought the Kingdom of God. When He ascended, He did not take it back with Him. He sent His Spirit to empower us to perpetuate His Kingdom here on earth. This is the same Spirit who moved on the waters in Genesis 1; the same Spirit who brought things into existence from nothing when God said, *"Let there be...."* That is the power that lives inside us as sons of God.

Genesis 1:26 is a key verse to understanding who we are in Christ:

"Then God said, 'Let us make mankind in our image, in our likeness...'"

If we are made like God, with the same Spirit living in us, then we possess the same ability to speak things into existence.

If there is a faith that can say to a mountain, "Move," and it be removed, the real problems in our lives are not the mountains, but our faith or lack thereof. Elijah was a man like us, and he said, "No rain." There was no rain for three years until he spoke again that there would be rain.

Joshua was a man like us, and he said, "Sun, stand still over Gibeon, and you, moon, over the Valley of Aijalon." If you understand science, you will know that for that to happen the entire universe had to stop moving.

One man did that.

Your tongue is a weapon of mass destruction. Everything you utter from your mouth should be based on your agreement with heaven. The problem we have in the church is that we use our tongue to advance the kingdom of darkness and not the Kingdom of God. We are quick to utter the negative while subjecting the positive to skepticism and scrutiny.

If the church is going to move from our traditional roots to a glorious Church that will continue to perpetuate the Kingdom of God as we read about in Acts, we need first to understand who we really are. We are a people who can call forth something out of nothing.

Faith speaks things that are not, as if they are. Let the weak say, "I am strong." Let the poor say, "I am rich." Let the sick say, "I am healed."

When we understand who we are, we will speak right. Secondly, we need to see from a proper perspective.

"And God raised us up with Christ and seated us with him in the heavenly realms in Christ Jesus." - Ephesians 2:6

Presently, we exist in two realms: the earthly and the heavenly. Right now, we are seated with Christ in heavenly places. A good friend of mine always said, "We are special, because angels have to stand and bow, but we are seated with Christ." Most Christians live their lives from the perspective of earth to heaven. We see ourselves on this long, difficult journey. "If I can just barely make it to heaven; if I can just somehow make it to heaven…" Beloved, we are already in heaven.

"And I saw a new heaven and a new earth: for the first heaven and the first earth were passed away; and there was no more sea. And I John saw the holy city, New Jerusalem, coming down from God out of heaven, prepared as a bride adorned for her husband." - Revelation 21: 1-2

God's ultimate purpose for man is to rule the earth and, by extension, all creation. In doing so, His heart has always been to dwell with man. He has done everything possible to make this a reality. Salvation was never about us trying to reach God.

"…but God demonstrates His own love towards us, in that while we were yet sinners, Christ died for us." - Romans 5:8

We must get the perspective right. We must understand what

Christ did for us and live out that reality. He has washed us, cleansed us, perfected us and put us to sit with Him in heavenly places.

"...in this world, we are like Jesus." - 1 John 4:17

If we live our lives from the perspective of earth to heaven, then principalities, powers, rulers of the darkness of this world and spiritual wickedness will always be above us, and we will never gain victory over them or live in the glory of God's presence.

If we live from a proper perspective of heaven to earth, where we are not sick, we lack nothing, the Kingdom of God is active and alive, and what we say has the power to change reality, to stop the rain, to freeze the universe, to raise even the dead…We can live from a proper perspective of heaven to earth with principalities, powers, rulers of darkness, spiritual wickedness in high places below our feet.

"...we will trample on snakes and scorpions and overcome ALL the power of the enemy, and nothing will harm us." - Luke 10:19

"...we will declare a thing, and it shall be done." - Job 22:28

"...we will say to our mountains, move…and it will be removed and cast into the sea." - Mark 11:23

We will have authority to deliver our people from demonic

oppression and possession. We will say to demons, "Go walk in the dry places" and they must obey.

We will say to our bodies, *"...by His stripes you are healed"* and our bodies must obey (See Isaiah 53:5 & 1 Peter 2:24).

"For there is a name that is above every name, and at the name of Jesus every knee should bow, in heaven and on earth and under the earth, and every tongue confess that Jesus Christ is Lord." - Philippians 2:9

If we get the perspective right and live from heaven to earth, everything that bows to Jesus bows to us. What do you have in your soul? God has given you the kingdom, keys, and the Holy Spirit. We must get the perspective right.

This is the Word from God through me to every member of this church: When your earthly position comes in alignment with your heavenly position, you will become like Jesus Christ in this earth. Your family will change. Your community will change. Your church will change.

There are some things we need to deal with as a church. The first is the sin issue. We get one opportunity (this lifetime) to master sin. If we fail now, we fail for all eternity.

"If you do what is right, will you not be accepted? But if you do not do what is right, sin is crouching at your door; it desires to have you, but you must rule over it." - Genesis 4:7

C. Orville McLeish

I had a dream in which I was running and walking around a church that was filled with filth. It was a picture of what is going on in today's churches. The level of sin in the church has reached an all-time high. People are living double lives and following the thoughts of their carnal hearts. Marriages are falling apart, accessing porn and engaging in masturbation are normal practices, and people tell lies to protect their egos. We have much to repent for and turn from if we are willing to face our own morality and expose ourselves to the purifying fire of God. There is no glory without repentance.

The second issue the church needs to address is the faith issue. It is not something we talk about, but something we live. I have had a challenge taking medication, even when there is something wrong with me. I have a deep conviction that it is contradictory to claim faith while putting much confidence in medicine. It feels like I am sending a message that Jesus' sacrifice was not enough to heal me. I now live at the place where I will put my life on the line to believe God. Are you willing to die for the cause of the true gospel?

"This Good News tells us how God makes us right in his sight. This is accomplished from start to finish by faith. As the Scriptures say, 'It is through faith that a righteous person has life.'" - Romans 1:17

The glorious Church is a living, breathing epistle that lives and walks by faith, and not just preaches and teaches about it. Our lives must reflect our personal inner conviction of God in our lives. He gives revelation, and we must be bold enough to live it. Faith is stepping off a boat, knowing that God will not let you sink.

The third and final issue is the fear issue. Anything you fear is a weapon of torture in the hands of the enemy. Have you ever had a condition that no doctor can diagnose? All sickness has its origin in the spiritual realm. The greatest weapon the enemy has in his arsenal is fear, which is a faith-killer, a vision-killer and ultimately can lead to an untimely death. We must conquer fear in order to become the glorious Church.

"For the Spirit God gave us does not make us timid, but gives us power, love and self-discipline." - 2 Timothy 1:7

Prophetic Word

This is a time of refreshing for My church when the true sons of God will rise up and take their rightful place. They will overcome the world, death and the enemy, ultimately placing him under the souls of their feet. That is the purpose for the church. As I have overcome the world, the devil, and death, so must each one of you overcome. I have shown you how so just go and get it done. Stop making excuses. Stop hiding behind others, and reasons, traditions and rituals. You are not escaping but denying the world what it really needs. Who will set the captives free, if not you? Who will heal the sick, raise the dead and cast out demons, if not you? The time for my sons to manifest has finally come. Look around you, and you will see the manifestations happening in epic proportions and spreading widely and rapidly. You are a part of My church, and the gates of hades will not prevail against you. You are My glorious ones. You have been chosen for such a time as this.

CHAPTER FOURTEEN
As He Is So Are You

We are created in the image of God, yet faced with the epidemic of Identity Crisis in the present age. It seems as though the fall of the first man was just the beginning of a perpetual event. The degradation of morality in today's society is high, and I want to believe that some of us are sensitive enough to heed the call of God's nature within us, to become the solution.

This book was written to ignite a desire within us, to engage in pursuit of God's agenda for the generations of present time.

Isaiah 60 speaks of darkness covering the earth, but it also made a wonderful declaration:

"For behold, the darkness shall cover the earth, and deep darkness the people; but the Lord will arise over you, and His glory will be seen upon you. The Gentiles shall come to your light, and kings to the brightness of your rising." - Isaiah 60:2-3

It would not be prudent of us to be so much focused on the darkness that we miss out on manifesting the light. We are the light of the world (See Matthew 5:14-16). Yes, the world needs Jesus; and those who carry the fullness of the God-head are the ones carrying what the world needs. You are the cure. You are the solution. Unless we see ourselves as one with God, we will miss out on the simple truth that can change this world: we are the carriers of light and it is our responsibility to dispel the darkness that is covering the earth.

While contemplating the content for this chapter, one of my favorite cousins was shot and killed. The circumstances surrounding his murder is still unclear, but it is believed that the bullet was not even intended for him, but it took his life. The daily news shows an increase in sexual abuse, murders, scamming, prostitution, revenge killings, suicides and a myriad of problems being faced by communities and families alike. Every single day somebody's world is unexpectedly turned upside down by some man-made tragedy of sorts.

The community close to where I live is known for roadside prostitution. The women stand by the side of the road, displaying their products and seeking to pick up their next customer. This is their means of catering for the needs of their children, themselves and surviving the demands of our escalating economy.

There is an exponential increase in technology. The means of communication has improved to the point where anyone, anywhere in the world, can instantly become your neighbor. The WhatsApp craze has dimmed the lines of communication; and while it makes it easy for people to communicate, there is also an increase in extramarital affairs as it is now easy to build and foster "other" relationships. There is hardly any need for face to face engagement anymore, unless it is of a sexual nature.

I have also observed the aggression within our young people. Fatal fights are breaking out amongst youth in schools and everywhere. Sadly, the motive behind the fights is often not something to die for. It is in the hearts of men that the alchemy of life is first formulated then released into the world. The Bible says it this way:

Keep your heart with all diligence, for out of it spring the issues of life. - Proverbs 4:23 – NKJV

This therefore means that the darkness which covers the earth springs from the hearts of men. The only countermeasure to this darkness, therefore, is the light of Christ beaming from the heart of a believer. It is only this beam of love and hope that can dispel the darkness upon the earth. In other words, man is the problem and within man lies the solution to the problem.

For centuries, the church has sidestepped the responsibility of fixing the earth. As a matter of fact, the church has, for a long time, perceived itself on earth as a mere passer-by on the way to divine eternity. We remain stiff-necked against taking our rightful position of dominion on earth. We have buried our heads in the sand of non-Biblical traditions that bear no impact. We attend church always with the expectation to receive something, but never to give something. Even when we give, we still expect to receive a pat on the back in the very least! The light within us, therefore, remains truncated. It is like an undeveloped and uncultivated seed, bearing much potential, but manifesting no impact. It is no wonder the church has been reduced to an object of ridicule instead of being the glorious authority on earth!

"You are the salt of the earth; but if the salt loses its flavor, how shall it be seasoned? It is then good for nothing but to be thrown out and trampled underfoot by men." - Matthew 5:13

Many churches are dying because they have lost their relevance in a fast-changing society. Young people cannot relate to the church much, because the church remains aloof from their struggles and issues. They have sub-consciously learnt to detach their day to day reality from church, hence living a double life.

Homosexuality and adultery are common practice, even on the pulpits. It is easy to live a fragmented life, while serving in church ministry, rising speedily through the ranks of church leadership unchallenged, unrepentant and without conviction. It would seem like people are becoming more like animals than human beings. We are drifting further and further away from an identity given to us by the One who created us in His image and likeness. People have assumed an identity based on the fallen nature of man, and not on the WORD OF GOD. This has established an anti-humanity consciousness that is quite prevalent in our age, which a lot of believers stay in denial about.

The reality is, Man was created with the potential for both good and evil. Eve sinned via deception. Adam made a conscious choice; he did not have a conversation with the devil. There are two distinct natures at work in every human being:

"For we know that the law is spiritual, but I am carnal, sold under sin. For what I am doing, I do not understand. For what I will to do, that I do not practice; but what I hate, that I do. If, then, I do what I will not to do, I agree with the law that *it is* good. But now, *it is* no longer I who do it, but sin that dwells in me. For I know that in me (that is, in my flesh) nothing good dwells; for to will is present with me, but *how* to perform what is good I do not find. For the good that I will *to do,* I do not do; but the evil I will not *to do,* that I practice. Now if I do what I will not *to do,* it is no longer I who do it, but sin that dwells in me. I find then a law, that evil is present with me, the one who wills to do good. For I delight in the law of God according to the inward man. But I see another law in my members, warring against the law of my mind, and bringing me into captivity to the law of sin which is in my members. O wretched man that I am! Who will deliver me from this body of death? I thank God—through Jesus Christ our Lord! So then, with the mind I myself serve the law of God, but with the flesh the law of sin." - Romans 7:14-25 – NKJV

Jesus came to save our souls (See 1 Peter 1:8-12), so our soul is made new when we say yes to Jesus. If any man is in Christ, he is a new creature (See 2 Corinthians 5:17). Our spirit is perfect, because it is the breath of God. The record of sin and corruption resides in our flesh and continues to wrestle with our spirit, until the body is transfigured and glorified. We must acknowledge this inner war in order to avoid being fragmented. What is fragmentation? Fragmentation, in this context, is when a Christian is living a double life. On one hand, he is an upstanding member of the church, on the other hand, he is a practicing homosexual, adulterer, wife beater, child abuser, etc. Unfortunately, I see a lot of this in the church.

This inner battle is real, and no one is exempt from it. Good and evil exists in all of us. In my professional experience, for instance, I have found that Christians are some of the worst people to work for. I am convinced that the perception of Christianity, by the Christian, needs redemption. I don't even like using the title anymore. We backbite, gossip, tear down at one another; we don't support each other; we are hostile, critical; filled with pride, selfishness and a false humility that I find utterly annoying, yet I know the value of people, and I know all this is an issue of identity because we don't know who we are. Those who know who they are function differently. A superhero who does not know his identity will not function like a superhero; he will live just like any other ordinary man. We don't know who we are; this is why we do the things that we shouldn't do; and we don't do the things we should do.

There are pleasures this world has to offer, but if you want to walk in the fullness of what God has for you, you must deny yourself those pleasures. The question is, "Is it worth the sacrifice?"

Paul says:

"I affirm, by the boasting in you which I have in Christ Jesus our Lord, I die daily." - 1 Corinthians 15:21

To die daily is to make a conscious choice that God is worth giving up some things for. If you try to get the best of both worlds, you diminish who you are; you suppress the greater that is within you.

In acknowledging this inner war, we must then decide who we want to be. Do you want to be identified with Christ or do you want to be identified with the world and the systems of the world? You can't have both; light and darkness cannot co-exist.

If you are going to be an unrepentant adulterer, fornicator, homosexual, liar, thief, do it full time. Don't waste time in church. I see so many serving God, but their chosen identity is based on their sins, weaknesses, inadequacies, lack, people's opinion, their background and upbringing, educational background or lack thereof, etc. NONE OF THESE things define you. Only God can define you, because He made you. For instance, if God says you can do all things, then you can do all things! If this does not manifest in your life, it is because your faith is limited; it means your own sight is too short to see beyond the present physical manifestation of your life issues.

In order to change your life, you must change what you believe about yourself. What you think about God is even far more important than what you think about yourself. What we think about God is usually not very accurate, because we try to pull Him down to our level. I submit to you today that the one who doesn't know God, doesn't know himself, because He gave you His identity and nature.

The following is a fresh translation from the Coptic text published by Messrs. Brill of Leiden:

> *These are the secret words which the living Jesus spoke, and Didymus Judas Thomas wrote them down. Jesus said: If those who lead you say unto you: Behold, the Kingdom is in heaven, then the birds of the heaven will be before you. If they say unto you: It is in the sea, then the fish will be before you. But the Kingdom is within you, and it is outside of you. When you know yourselves, then shall you be known, and you shall know that you are the sons of the living Father. But if ye do not know yourselves, then you are in poverty, and you are poverty.*[3]

God did not make us for sin, and He did not make us sinners. We did that.

"Who told you that you were naked?" the LORD God asked. "Have you eaten from the tree whose fruit I commanded you not to eat?" - Genesis 3:11 - NLT

---

[3] The Gospel of Thomas

A Glorious Church

Our identity is often based on what we have been told; so, I want to tell you who you really are. We have preached so many messages about God, beautiful messages. But we haven't preached a lot of messages about us, except that we are worms, wretches, unworthy, nothing, just a low down, dirty, good for nothing sinner, etc. Let's talk about God. I agree that He will never leave or forsake you. He will always be with you, even to the ends of the earth. He will come through for you when you need Him. He is a Provider, a Banner over me, a Shield and Buckler, a Present Help in times of trouble, Healer, Deliverer, Friend to the friendless, and Shelter to the Homeless.

Now let's talk about you:

What is man that You are mindful of him, and the son of man that You visit him? For You have made him a little lower than the angels, and You have crowned him with glory and honor. You have made him to have dominion over the works of Your hands; You have put all things under his feet. - Psalm 8:4-6 - NKJV

What are the works of God's hands? All creation. We preach about God, but we don't assume His nature. We preach about God, but we don't assume His identity. With all the knowledge we have about God, we fail to be able to change anyone's circumstance; we fail to be world changers; we fail to be the answer to someone's prayer.

"Assuredly, I say to you, among those born of women there has not risen one greater than John the Baptist; but he who is least

in the kingdom of heaven is greater than he." - Matthew 11:11 - NKJV

"You are of God, little children, and have overcome them, because He who is in you is greater than he who is in the world." - 1 John 4:4 - NKJV

There is a greater version of you inside you. God meticulously designed you for a great purpose in service to humanity. Like David expresses it, God knitted/formed you in your mother's womb (See Psalm 139:13). You are God's idea; He is your Father; He gave you an identity. Do not throw your real identity out of the window for a lesser you.

God has endowed you with three of the most powerful forces on earth: hope, faith and love. You don't have to choose to settle for status quo. It is hope that causes us to think and imagine something different from what we may be subjected to at the moment. We can pursue hope, knowing that there is something better, but we must be willing to give our lives for what we believe. We must believe that we can make a difference, and it is hope that enables us to see that there is something more. We must become love and be willing to die to self, so that others can partake in the dream we have of a better world.

I realized late in life that while growing up, church doctrine damaged my thinking. We talk a lot about the rapture, and Jesus' eminent return and it robbed me of hope. So, when I wanted to start gym, I was dissuaded because I thought by the time I got the results I wanted, Jesus would have returned. Then

I questioned the relevance of going to college. I was thinking, "What would be the point of hassling through college if the world will end in five years?" If I knew then, what I know now, I would have studied to become a Scientist or a Doctor so I could make a higher contribution to humanity and repairing the breaches on Earth. I learned enough from my own experience to know that I must be careful how I portray God to the younger generation. It is not good for their young, developing minds to see the world only from the perspective of judgment, wrath and destruction.

Martin Luther King said, "I have a dream…" He was willing to die for that dream. What is your dream? What kind of world are you building for your children? What would happen if you made up your mind to leave a mark in creation that you were here? What legacy are you leaving behind? How have you impacted your community? Did you invent something new? Did you start a business that the next generation can benefit from? Why not write a book? Write a new praise and worship song! Do something! God put you on earth for a reason. He gave His only Son for you; He gave you His Holy Spirit; He empowered you; He gave you the keys to the kingdom. Do you realize that the one who holds the keys to the kingdom has power and authority over this world?

If Adam gave up the keys when he fell, and Jesus came to restore all that was lost and he took the keys back and gave the keys to you, there is a new ruler in town. That is why God is King of kings and Lord of lords, because you are a king and a lord.

"But you are a chosen generation, a royal priesthood, a holy nation, His own special people, that you may proclaim the praises of Him who called you out of darkness into His marvelous light." - 1 Peter 2:9 - NKJV

I love John's take on it. Just one line of Scripture, and if you are not careful you will miss the point:

"Love has been perfected among us in this: that we may have boldness in the day of judgment; because as He is, so are we in this world." - 1 John 4:17

I believe this is the real journey of Christianity; for the light, love and image of God in man to be restored to its original intensity and impact. If we become partakers of God's divine nature, as Paul states, then it means we can also assume our rightful dominion over the earth with absolute conviction and confidence:

"The Spirit of the Lord God is upon Me, because the Lord has anointed Me to preach good tidings to the poor; He has sent me to heal the brokenhearted, to proclaim liberty to the captives, and to open the prison for those who are bound; to proclaim the acceptable year of the Lord, and the day of vengeance of our God; to comfort all who mourn, to console those who mourn in Zion, to give them beauty for ashes, the oil of joy for mourning, the garment of praise for the spirit of heaviness; that they may be called trees of righteousness, the planting of the Lord, that He may be glorified. And they shall rebuild the old ruins, they shall raise up the former

desolations, and they shall repair the ruined cities, the desolations of many generations." - Isaiah 61:1-4 - NKJV

There is work to be done on Earth; the greater in you must arise. Buy land, build houses, start a farm, get married, have children, start a business, get that career; God has made you a force to recon within creation. What will you be remembered for when you leave the dimensions of the Earth into eternity? Did you fulfill your divine call and destiny? We all came into this world with a scroll written in heaven about us, regarding what we are assigned to accomplish. What will people be saying about you three years after you are gone? How will the generations to come benefit from the life you are living now?

If you are satisfied with what the church and the world is; if you adhere to the status quo and you don't have a cause that you are willing to die for, then this call is not for you. You will die and not be remembered much. However, if you want your name inscribed in creation long after your departure, then it is imperative that you embrace the greater that is in you. I urge you to embrace the identity that God has given you; be willing to accept the responsibilities that accompany your calling and make that step of faith and do something great with your life. By so doing, and with much shameless persistence and tenacity, we will begin to see the emergence of the glorious Church on the Earth, and the darkness will be replaced with a piercing beam of glorious light: that light, dearest reader, is you.

Conclusion

I end with the words of Joel. I believe this Word speaks to a time that is yet to come, though we have tasted of it, to some measure, through the centuries that followed Christ ascension:

Blow the trumpet in Zion, and sound an alarm in My holy mountain! Let all the inhabitants of the land tremble; for the day of the Lord is coming, for it is at hand: a day of darkness and gloominess, a day of clouds and thick darkness, like the morning clouds spread over the mountains. A people come, great and strong, the like of whom has never been; nor will there ever be any such after them, even for many successive generations. A fire devours before them, and behind them a flame burns; the land is like the Garden of Eden before them, and behind them a desolate wilderness; surely nothing shall escape them. Their appearance is like the appearance of horses; and like swift steeds, so they run. With a noise like chariots over mountaintops they leap, like the noise of a flaming fire that devours the stubble, like a strong people set in battle array. Before them the people writhe in pain; all faces are drained of color. They run like mighty men, they climb the wall like men of war; every one marches in formation, and they do not break ranks. They do not push one another; every one marches in his own column. Though they lunge between the weapons, they are not cut down. They run to and fro in the city, they run on the wall; they climb into the houses, they enter at the windows like a thief. The earth quakes before them, the heavens tremble; the sun and moon grow dark, and the stars diminish their brightness. The Lord gives voice before His army, for His camp is very great; for strong is the One who executes His word. For the day of the Lord is great and very terrible; who can endure it? "Now, therefore," says the Lord, "Turn to Me with all your heart, with fasting, with weeping, and with mourning." So rend your heart, and not your garments; return to the Lord your God, for He is gracious and merciful, slow to anger, and of great kindness; and He relents from doing harm. Who knows if He will turn and relent, and leave a blessing behind Him— A grain offering and a drink offering for the Lord your God? Blow the trumpet in Zion, consecrate a fast, call a sacred assembly; gather the people, sanctify the congregation, assemble the elders, gather the children and nursing babes; let the bridegroom go out from his chamber, and the bride from her dressing room. Let the priests, who minister to the Lord, weep between the porch and the altar; let them say, "Spare Your people, O Lord, and do not give Your heritage to reproach, that the nations should rule over them. Why should they say among the peoples, 'Where is their God?'" Then the Lord will be zealous for His land, and pity His people. The Lord will answer and say to His people, "Behold, I will send you grain and new wine and oil, and you will be satisfied by them; I will no longer make you a reproach among the nations. But I will remove far from you the northern army, and will drive him away into a barren and desolate land,

A Glorious Church

with his face toward the eastern sea and his back toward the western sea; his stench will come up, and his foul odor will rise, because he has done monstrous things." Fear not, O land; be glad and rejoice, for the Lord has done marvelous things! Do not be afraid, you beasts of the field; for the open pastures are springing up, and the tree bears its fruit; the fig tree and the vine yield their strength. Be glad then, you children of Zion, and rejoice in the Lord your God; for He has given you the former rain faithfully, and He will cause the rain to come down for you—the former rain, and the latter rain in the first month. The threshing floors shall be full of wheat, and the vats shall overflow with new wine and oil. "So I will restore to you the years that the swarming locust has eaten, the crawling locust, the consuming locust, and the chewing locust, my great army which I sent among you. You shall eat in plenty and be satisfied, and praise the name of the Lord your God, who has dealt wondrously with you; and My people shall never be put to shame. Then you shall know that I am in the midst of Israel: I am the Lord your God and there is no other. My people shall never be put to shame. "And it shall come to pass afterward that I will pour out My Spirit on all flesh; your sons and your daughters shall prophesy, your old men shall dream dreams, your young men shall see visions. And also on My menservants and on My maidservants I will pour out My Spirit in those days. "And I will show wonders in the heavens and in the earth: blood and fire and pillars of smoke. The sun shall be turned into darkness, and the moon into blood, before the coming of the great and awesome day of the Lord. And it shall come to pass that whoever calls on the name of the Lord shall be saved. For in Mount Zion and in Jerusalem there shall be deliverance,

as the Lord has said, among the remnant whom the Lord calls.
- Joel 2:1-32 - NKJV

www.ingramcontent.com/pod-product-compliance
Lightning Source LLC
Chambersburg PA
CBHW072009110526
44592CB00012B/1246